SOUPS

and

BREADS

Publications International, Ltd.

Microwave Cooking: Microwave ovens vary in wattage. Use the cooking times as guidelines and check for doneness before adding more time.

WARNING: Food preparation, baking and cooking involve inherent dangers: misuse of electric products, sharp electric tools, boiling water, hot stoves, allergic reactions, foodborne illnesses and the like, pose numerous potential risks. Publications International, Ltd. (PIL) assumes no responsibility or liability for any damages you may experience as a result of following recipes, instructions, tips or advice in this publication.

While we hope this publication helps you find new ways to eat delicious foods, you may not always achieve the results desired due to variations in ingredients, cooking temperatures, typos, errors, omissions or individual cooking abilities.

Let's get social!

@Publications_International
@PublicationsInternational
www.pilbooks.com

CONTENTS

SOUPS

BREADS

SOUPS

MEATY MAIN-DISH SOUPS

HEARTY VEGETABLE SOUPS

PASTA and NOODLE SOUPS

BEAN and GRAIN SOUPS

MEATY MAIN-DISH SOUPS

SAUSAGE AND LENTIL SOUP
Makes 4 to 6 servings

8 ounces bulk hot Italian sausage

1 onion, chopped

2 cloves garlic, minced

1 stalk celery, chopped

1 carrot, chopped

1 small zucchini, chopped

3 to 3½ cups chicken broth, divided

1 can (about 14 ounces) diced tomatoes

1 cup dried lentils, rinsed and sorted

½ teaspoon salt

½ teaspoon dried oregano

½ teaspoon dried basil

¼ teaspoon dried thyme

¼ teaspoon black pepper

Chopped fresh basil and grated Parmesan cheese (optional)

1 Cook sausage in large saucepan or Dutch oven over medium-high heat 6 to 8 minutes or until browned, stirring to break up meat.

2 Add onion; cook and stir 3 minutes or until onion begins to soften. Add garlic; cook and stir 1 minute. Add celery, carrot and zucchini; cook 3 minutes, stirring occasionally.

3 Stir in 3 cups broth, tomatoes, lentils, salt, oregano, dried basil, thyme and pepper; bring to a boil. Reduce heat to low; cover and simmer about 1 hour or until lentils are tender. Add additional broth, if necessary, to thin soup. Garnish with fresh basil and cheese.

7

CHICKEN ENCHILADA SOUP

Makes 8 to 10 servings

- 2 tablespoons vegetable oil, divided
- 1½ pounds boneless skinless chicken breasts, cut into ½-inch pieces
- ½ cup chopped onion
- 2 cloves garlic, minced
- 2 cans (about 14 ounces each) chicken broth
- 3 cups water, divided
- 1 cup masa harina
- 1 package (16 ounces) pasteurized process cheese product, cubed
- 1 can (10 ounces) mild red enchilada sauce
- 1 teaspoon chili powder
- ½ teaspoon salt
- ½ teaspoon ground cumin
- 1 large tomato, seeded and chopped
- Crispy tortilla strips*

If tortilla strips are not available, crumble tortilla chips into bite-size pieces.

1 Heat 1 tablespoon oil in large saucepan or Dutch oven over medium-high heat. Add chicken; cook and stir 10 minutes or until no longer pink. Transfer to medium bowl with slotted spoon; drain any excess liquid from saucepan.

2 Heat remaining 1 tablespoon oil in same saucepan over medium-high heat. Add onion and garlic; cook and stir 3 minutes or until softened. Stir in broth.

3 Whisk 2 cups water into masa harina in large bowl until smooth. Whisk mixture into broth in saucepan. Stir in remaining 1 cup water, cheese product, enchilada sauce, chili powder, salt and cumin; bring to a boil over high heat. Stir in chicken.

4 Reduce heat to medium-low; simmer 30 minutes, stirring frequently. Top with tomato and tortilla strips.

BEEF VEGETABLE SOUP
Makes 6 to 8 servings

1½ pounds cubed beef
    stew meat

¼ cup all-purpose flour

3 tablespoons vegetable oil,
    divided

1 onion, chopped

2 stalks celery, chopped

3 tablespoons tomato paste

2 teaspoons salt

1 teaspoon dried thyme

½ teaspoon garlic powder

¼ teaspoon black pepper

6 cups beef broth, divided

1 can (28 ounces) stewed
    tomatoes, undrained

1 tablespoon Worcestershire
    sauce

1 bay leaf

4 unpeeled red potatoes
    (about 1 pound), cut
    into 1-inch pieces

3 medium carrots, cut
    in half lengthwise and
    cut into ½-inch slices

6 ounces green beans,
    trimmed and cut
    into 1-inch pieces

1 cup frozen corn

1 Combine beef and flour in medium bowl; toss to coat. Heat 1 tablespoon oil in large saucepan or Dutch oven over medium-high heat. Cook beef in two batches 5 minutes or until browned, adding additional 1 tablespoon oil after first batch. Remove beef to medium bowl.

2 Heat remaining 1 tablespoon oil in same saucepan. Add onion and celery; cook and stir 5 minutes or until softened. Add tomato paste, salt, thyme, garlic powder and pepper; cook and stir 1 minute. Stir in 1 cup broth, scraping up browned bits from bottom of saucepan. Stir in remaining 5 cups broth, tomatoes with juice, Worcestershire sauce, bay leaf and beef; bring to a boil.

3 Reduce heat to low; cover and simmer 1 hour and 20 minutes. Add potatoes and carrots; simmer 15 minutes.

4 Add green beans and corn; cook 12 minutes or until vegetables are tender. Remove and discard bay leaf.

CREAMY CRAB CHOWDER
Makes 6 to 8 servings

1 tablespoon butter

1 cup finely chopped onion

2 cloves garlic, minced

1 cup finely chopped celery

½ cup finely chopped
   green bell pepper

½ cup finely chopped
   red bell pepper

3 cans (about 14 ounces
   each) chicken broth

3 cups diced peeled
   potatoes

1 package (10 ounces)
   frozen corn

2 cans (6½ ounces each)
   lump crabmeat

½ cup half-and-half

¼ teaspoon black pepper

1 Melt butter in large saucepan or Dutch oven over medium heat. Add onion and garlic; cook and stir 6 minutes or until softened but not browned. Add celery and bell peppers; cook 8 minutes or until celery is tender, stirring frequently.

2 Stir in broth and potatoes; bring to a boil over high heat. Reduce heat to low; simmer 10 minutes. Add corn; cook 5 minutes or until potatoes are tender.

3 Drain crabmeat; place in small bowl. Flake to break up large pieces; add to soup. Stir in half-and-half and black pepper; cook over low heat just until heated through. (Do not boil.)

HEARTY TUSCAN SOUP
Makes 6 to 8 servings

1 teaspoon olive oil

1 pound bulk mild or hot
   Italian sausage*

1 medium onion, chopped

3 cloves garlic, minced

¼ cup all-purpose flour

5 cups chicken broth

1 teaspoon salt

½ teaspoon Italian seasoning

3 medium unpeeled russet
   potatoes (about
   1 pound), halved
   lengthwise and
   thinly sliced

2 cups packed torn
   stemmed kale leaves

1 cup half-and-half or
   whipping cream

*Or use sausage links and
remove from casings.*

1 Heat oil in large saucepan or Dutch oven over medium-high heat. Add sausage; cook 5 minutes or until sausage begins to brown, stirring to break up meat. Add onion and garlic; cook about 5 minutes or until onion is softened and sausage is browned, stirring occasionally.

2 Add flour; cook and stir 1 minute. Add broth, salt and Italian seasoning; bring to a boil. Stir in potatoes and kale. Reduce heat to medium-low; simmer 15 to 20 minutes or until potatoes are fork-tender.

3 Reduce heat to low; stir in half-and-half. Cook about 5 minutes or until heated through.

SKILLET CHICKEN SOUP
Makes 4 servings

1 teaspoon paprika

½ teaspoon salt

¼ teaspoon black pepper

12 ounces boneless skinless chicken breasts or thighs, cut into ¾-inch pieces

1 tablespoon vegetable oil

1 large onion, chopped

1 red bell pepper, cut into ½-inch pieces

3 cloves garlic, minced

3 cups chicken broth

1 can (19 ounces) cannellini beans or small white beans, rinsed and drained

3 cups sliced savoy or napa cabbage

½ cup herb-flavored croutons, slightly crushed (optional)

1 Combine paprika, salt and black pepper in medium bowl; mix well. Add chicken; toss to coat.

2 Heat oil in large skillet over medium-high heat. Add chicken, onion, bell pepper and garlic; cook and stir 8 minutes or until chicken is cooked through.

3 Add broth and beans; bring to a simmer. Reduce heat to medium-low; cover and simmer 5 minutes. Stir in cabbage; cover and simmer 3 minutes or until cabbage is wilted. Top with croutons, if desired.

Tip

Savoy cabbage is round with pale green crinkled leaves. Napa cabbage, also known as Chinese cabbage, is elongated with light green stalks.

CORNED BEEF AND CABBAGE SOUP

Makes about 8 servings

1 tablespoon vegetable oil

1 onion, chopped

2 stalks celery, chopped

2 carrots, chopped

2 cloves garlic, minced

4 to 5 cups coarsely chopped green cabbage (about half of small head)

12 ounces unpeeled Yukon gold potatoes, chopped

4 cups beef broth

4 cups water

½ cup quick-cooking barley

1 teaspoon salt

1 teaspoon dried thyme

½ teaspoon black pepper

¼ teaspoon ground mustard

12 ounces corned beef (leftovers or deli corned beef, about 2½ cups), cut into ½-inch pieces

1 Heat oil in large saucepan or Dutch oven over medium-high heat. Add onion, celery and carrots; cook 6 minutes or until vegetables are softened, stirring occasionally. Add garlic; cook and stir 1 minute.

2 Stir in cabbage, potatoes, broth, water, barley, salt, thyme, pepper and mustard; bring to a boil. Reduce heat to medium-low; simmer 20 minutes, stirring occasionally.

3 Stir in corned beef; cook 10 to 15 minutes or until potatoes are tender. Season with additional salt and pepper, if desired.

SOUTHWEST CORN AND TURKEY SOUP

Makes 6 servings

2 dried ancho chiles (about 4 inches long) *or* 6 dried New Mexico chiles (about 6 inches long)

1 tablespoon vegetable oil

1 medium onion, thinly sliced

3 cloves garlic, minced

1 teaspoon ground cumin

3 cans (about 14 ounces each) chicken broth

2 cups shredded cooked turkey

2 small zucchini, cut into ½-inch slices

1 can (about 15 ounces) black beans or chickpeas, rinsed and drained

1 package (10 ounces) frozen corn

¼ cup yellow cornmeal

1 teaspoon dried oregano

⅓ cup chopped fresh cilantro

1 Cut stems from chiles; remove and discard seeds. Place chiles in medium bowl; cover with boiling water. Let stand 20 to 40 minutes or until softened.

2 Drain chiles; cut open lengthwise and lay flat on work surface. Scrape chile pulp from skins with edge of small knife. Finely mince pulp; discard skins.

3 Heat oil in large saucepan or Dutch oven over medium heat. Add onion; cook and stir 3 minutes. Add garlic and cumin; cook and stir 30 seconds.

4 Stir in broth, reserved chile pulp, turkey, zucchini, beans, corn, cornmeal and oregano; bring to a boil over high heat. Reduce heat to low; simmer 15 minutes or until zucchini is tender. Stir in cilantro just before serving.

SAVORY SEAFOOD SOUP
Makes 4 servings

2½ cups water or chicken broth

1½ cups dry white wine

1 onion, chopped

½ red bell pepper, chopped

½ green bell pepper, chopped

1 clove garlic, minced

½ teaspoon salt

8 ounces halibut, cut into 1-inch pieces

8 ounces sea scallops, cut into halves

1 teaspoon dried thyme

Juice of ½ lime

Dash hot pepper sauce

Black pepper

1 Combine water, wine, onion, bell peppers, garlic and salt in large saucepan; bring to a boil over high heat. Reduce heat to medium-low; cover and simmer 15 minutes or until bell peppers are tender, stirring occasionally.

2 Add fish, scallops and thyme; cook 2 minutes or until fish and scallops turn opaque. Stir in lime juice and hot pepper sauce. Season with additional salt and black pepper.

PORK AND CABBAGE SOUP
Makes 6 servings

8 ounces pork loin, cut into ½-inch pieces

1 medium onion, chopped

2 slices bacon, finely chopped

1 can (about 28 ounces) whole tomatoes, drained and coarsely chopped

2 cups chicken broth

2 cups beef broth

2 medium carrots, sliced

1 teaspoon salt

1 bay leaf

¾ teaspoon dried marjoram

⅛ teaspoon black pepper

½ medium cabbage, chopped

2 tablespoons chopped fresh parsley

1 Combine pork, onion and bacon large saucepan or Dutch oven; cook and stir over medium heat 5 minutes or until pork is no longer pink and onion is slightly softened.

2 Stir in tomatoes, chicken broth, beef broth, carrots, salt, bay leaf, marjoram and pepper; bring to a boil over high heat. Reduce heat to medium-low; simmer 30 minutes. Remove and discard bay leaf.

3 Add cabbage; bring to a boil over high heat. Reduce heat to medium-low; simmer about 15 minutes or until cabbage is tender. Stir in parsley.

COCONUT CURRY CHICKEN SOUP
Makes 4 to 6 servings

3 cups chicken broth

8 boneless skinless chicken thighs

1 cup chopped onion, divided

1 teaspoon salt, divided

4 whole cloves

1 tablespoon butter

2 tablespoons curry powder

1¼ cups coconut milk

¼ cup plus 1 tablespoon chopped fresh mint, divided

3 tablespoons chopped crystallized ginger

¼ teaspoon ground cloves

1½ cups half-and-half

3 cups cooked rice (optional)

Lime wedges (optional)

1 Bring broth to a boil in large skillet over high heat. Add chicken, ½ cup onion, ½ teaspoon salt and whole cloves; return to a boil. Reduce heat to low; cover and simmer 40 minutes or until chicken is very tender.

2 Remove chicken to plate; set aside until cool enough to handle. Pour cooking liquid from skillet into glass measuring cup or bowl; discard onion and cloves.

3 Melt butter in same skillet over medium-high heat. Add remaining ½ cup onion; cook and stir 4 minutes or until onion is translucent. Add curry powder; cook and stir 20 seconds or just until fragrant.

4 Reduce heat to medium-low. Return cooking liquid to skillet with coconut milk, 1 tablespoon mint, ginger, ground cloves and remaining ½ teaspoon salt; cover and simmer 10 minutes.

5 Shred chicken into bite-size pieces. Add to soup with half-and-half; cook 3 minutes or until heated through. Sprinkle with remaining ¼ cup mint. Serve with rice and lime wedges, if desired.

BEEFY BROCCOLI AND CHEESE SOUP
Makes 4 servings

4 ounces ground beef

2 cups beef broth

1 package (10 ounces) frozen chopped broccoli, thawed

¼ cup chopped onion

1 cup milk

2 tablespoons all-purpose flour

½ teaspoon salt

1 cup (4 ounces) shredded sharp Cheddar cheese

1½ teaspoons chopped fresh oregano *or* ½ teaspoon dried oregano

Black pepper

Hot pepper sauce

1 Cook beef in medium saucepan over medium-high heat 6 to 8 minutes or until browned, stirring to break up meat. Drain fat; remove beef to medium bowl.

2 Add broth to saucepan; bring to a boil over medium-high heat. Add broccoli and onion; cook 5 minutes or until broccoli is tender.

3 Stir milk into flour in small bowl until smooth. Add milk mixture, beef and salt to saucepan; cook and stir until thickened and heated through.

4 Add cheese and oregano; cook and stir over low heat just until cheese is melted. Season with additional salt, black pepper and hot pepper sauce.

RUSTIC COUNTRY TURKEY SOUP
Makes 4 to 6 servings

2 tablespoons olive oil

1 cup chopped onion

¾ cup sliced carrots

4 ounces sliced mushrooms

1 teaspoon minced garlic

2 cans (about 14 ounces each) chicken broth

2 ounces uncooked rotini pasta

1 teaspoon dried thyme

½ teaspoon poultry seasoning

¼ teaspoon salt

⅛ teaspoon red pepper flakes

2 cups chopped cooked turkey

¼ cup chopped fresh parsley

1 Heat oil in large saucepan or Dutch oven over medium-high heat. Add onion and carrots; cook and stir 2 minutes. Add mushrooms; cook 2 minutes. Add garlic; cook and stir 30 seconds. Add broth; bring to a boil.

2 Stir in pasta, thyme, poultry seasoning, salt and red pepper flakes; return to a boil. Reduce heat to low; cover and simmer 8 minutes or until pasta is tender.

3 Stir in turkey; cook 2 minutes or until heated through. Add parsley; cover and let stand 5 minutes before serving.

SPICY THAI SHRIMP SOUP

Makes 4 servings

1 tablespoon vegetable oil

1 pound medium raw
   shrimp, peeled and
   deveined, shells
   reserved

1 jalapeño pepper,
   cut into slivers

1 tablespoon paprika

¼ teaspoon ground red
   pepper

4 cans (about 14 ounces
   each) chicken broth

1 (½-inch) strip *each*
   lemon and lime peel

1 can (15 ounces) straw
   mushrooms, drained

   Juice of 1 lemon

   Juice of 1 lime

2 tablespoons soy sauce

1 red Thai pepper or red
   jalapeño pepper *or*
   ¼ small red bell pepper,
   cut into strips

¼ cup fresh cilantro leaves

1 Heat oil in large skillet over medium-high heat.
   Add shrimp and jalapeño; cook and stir 1 minute.
   Add paprika and ground red pepper; cook and
   stir 1 minute or until shrimp are pink and opaque.
   Remove to medium bowl.

2 Add shrimp shells to skillet; cook and stir
   30 seconds. Add broth and lemon and lime
   peels; bring to a boil. Reduce heat to low;
   cover and simmer 15 minutes.

3 Remove and discard shells and peels with slotted
   spoon. Add mushrooms and shrimp to broth;
   bring to a boil over medium heat. Stir in lemon
   and lime juices, soy sauce and Thai pepper; cook
   until just heated through. Sprinkle with cilantro.
   Serve immediately.

SPICY SQUASH AND CHICKEN SOUP

Makes 4 servings

1 tablespoon vegetable oil

1 small onion, finely chopped

1 stalk celery, finely chopped

2 cups chicken broth

2 cups cubed peeled butternut or delicata squash (about 1 small)

1 can (about 14 ounces) diced tomatoes with green chiles

1 cup chopped cooked chicken

¾ teaspoon salt

½ teaspoon ground ginger

⅛ teaspoon ground cumin

⅛ teaspoon black pepper

2 teaspoons lime juice

Sprigs fresh parsley or cilantro (optional)

1 Heat oil in large saucepan over medium heat. Add onion and celery; cook and stir 5 minutes or until vegetables are tender. Stir in broth, squash, tomatoes, chicken, salt, ginger, cumin and pepper; bring to a boil.

2 Reduce heat to low; cover and simmer 30 minutes or until squash is tender.

3 Stir in lime juice. Garnish with parsley.

HEARTY VEGETABLE SOUPS

CREAMY TOMATO SOUP

Makes 6 servings

3 tablespoons olive oil, divided

2 tablespoons butter

1 large onion, finely chopped

2 cloves garlic, minced

2 teaspoons sugar

1 teaspoon salt

½ teaspoon dried oregano

2 cans (28 ounces each) peeled Italian plum tomatoes, undrained

4 cups ½-inch focaccia cubes (half of 9-ounce loaf)

½ teaspoon black pepper

½ cup whipping cream

1 Heat 2 tablespoons oil and butter in large saucepan or Dutch oven over medium-high heat. Add onion; cook and stir 5 minutes or until softened. Add garlic, sugar, salt and oregano; cook and stir 30 seconds. Stir in tomatoes with juice; bring to a boil. Reduce heat to medium-low; simmer 45 minutes, stirring occasionally.

2 Meanwhile, prepare croutons. Preheat oven to 350°F. Combine focaccia cubes, remaining 1 tablespoon oil and pepper in large bowl; toss to coat. Spread on large rimmed baking sheet. Bake 10 minutes or until bread cubes are golden brown.

3 Blend soup with hand-held immersion blender until smooth. (Or blend soup in batches in blender or food processor.) Stir in cream; cook until heated through. Serve soup topped with croutons.

SUMMER CORN CHOWDER
Makes 6 servings

5 ears corn, shucked

2 tablespoons butter

1 medium onion, chopped

1 large poblano pepper, diced (¼-inch pieces)

2 cloves garlic, minced

4 cups chicken or vegetable broth

1½ teaspoons salt, divided

½ teaspoon black pepper, divided

¼ teaspoon ground red pepper

1 pound red potatoes, peeled and cut into ½-inch pieces

3 plum tomatoes, diced (about 2 cups)

½ cup whipping cream

2 tablespoons lime juice

2 tablespoons chopped fresh cilantro

¼ cup crumbled crisp-cooked bacon (optional)

1 Cut kernels off cobs; place in medium bowl. Working over bowl, run back of knife up and down cobs to release additional corn pulp and milk from cobs into bowl. Break cobs in half; set aside.

2 Melt butter in large saucepan or Dutch oven over medium heat. Add onion, poblano pepper and garlic; cook about 5 minutes or until vegetables are softened, stirring occasionally. Stir in broth, 1 teaspoon salt, ¼ teaspoon black pepper and red pepper; mix well. Add corn cobs; bring to a boil. Reduce heat to medium-low; cover and simmer 15 minutes.

3 Stir in potatoes; cover and simmer 20 minutes. Stir in corn and tomatoes; simmer, uncovered, 20 minutes.

4 Remove and discard corn cobs. Coarsely mash soup with potato masher. (Or use hand-held immersion blender to briefly blend soup just until slightly chunky.)

5 Stir in cream; cook 3 minutes or until heated through. Stir in lime juice, cilantro, remaining ½ teaspoon salt and ¼ teaspoon black pepper. Garnish with bacon.

WEST AFRICAN PEANUT SOUP
Makes 6 to 8 servings

2 tablespoons vegetable oil

1 large onion, chopped

½ cup chopped roasted peanuts

1½ tablespoons minced fresh ginger

4 cloves garlic, minced

1 teaspoon salt

4 cups vegetable broth

2 sweet potatoes, peeled and cut into ½-inch pieces

1 can (28 ounces) whole tomatoes, drained and coarsely chopped

¼ teaspoon ground red pepper

1 bunch Swiss chard or kale, stemmed and shredded

⅓ cup unsweetened peanut butter (creamy or chunky)

1 Heat oil in large saucepan or Dutch oven over medium-high heat. Add onion; cook and stir 5 minutes or until softened. Add peanuts, ginger, garlic and salt; cook and stir 1 minute. Stir in broth, sweet potatoes, tomatoes and red pepper; bring to a boil. Reduce heat to medium; simmer 10 minutes.

2 Stir in chard and peanut butter; cook over medium-low heat 10 minutes or until vegetables are tender and soup is creamy.

ROASTED POBLANO SOUP

Makes 4 servings

6 large poblano peppers

1 tablespoon olive oil

¾ cup chopped onion

½ cup thinly sliced celery

½ cup thinly sliced carrots

1 clove garlic, minced

2 cans (about 14 ounces each) vegetable broth

½ teaspoon salt

1 package (8 ounces) cream cheese, cubed

Black pepper

1 Preheat broiler. Line broiler pan or baking sheet with foil. Place poblano peppers on pan; broil 5 to 6 inches from heat source 15 minutes or until peppers are blistered and beginning to char, turning occasionally. Place peppers in medium bowl; cover with plastic wrap to steam and loosen skins. Let stand 20 minutes.

2 Meanwhile, heat oil in large saucepan over medium-high heat. Add onion, celery, carrots and garlic; cook and stir 4 minutes or until onion is translucent. Stir in broth and salt; bring to a boil. Reduce heat to medium-low; cover and simmer 12 minutes or until celery is tender.

3 Remove skins, stems and seeds from peppers. Briefly run peppers under cold water to help remove skins and seeds, if necessary. (This removes some smoky flavor, so work quickly.) Add peppers and cream cheese to broth mixture in saucepan.

4 Blend soup with hand-held immersion blender until smooth. (Or blend soup in batches in blender or food processor.) Cook and stir soup over medium heat 2 minutes or until heated through. Season with additional salt and black pepper.

GARDEN VEGETABLE SOUP
Makes 8 to 10 servings

1 tablespoon olive oil

1 medium onion, chopped

1 carrot, chopped

1 stalk celery, chopped

1 medium zucchini, diced

1 medium yellow squash, diced

1 red bell pepper, diced

2 tablespoons tomato paste

2 cloves garlic, minced

2 teaspoons salt

1 teaspoon Italian seasoning

½ teaspoon black pepper

8 cups vegetable broth

1 can (28 ounces) whole tomatoes, chopped, juice reserved

½ cup uncooked pearl barley

1 cup cut green beans (1-inch pieces)

½ cup corn

¼ cup slivered fresh basil

1 tablespoon lemon juice

1 Heat oil in large saucepan or Dutch oven over medium-high heat. Add onion, carrot and celery; cook and stir 6 minutes or until vegetables are softened.

2 Add zucchini, yellow squash and bell pepper; cook and stir 5 minutes or until softened. Stir in tomato paste, garlic, salt, Italian seasoning and black pepper; cook 1 minute. Stir in broth and tomatoes with juice; bring to a boil. Stir in barley.

3 Reduce heat to low; simmer 30 minutes. Stir in green beans and corn; cook 15 minutes or until barley is tender and green beans are crisp-tender. Stir in basil and lemon juice.

CREAMY SWEET POTATO SOUP

Makes 3 to 4 servings

4 cups water

1 pound sweet potatoes, peeled and cut into 1-inch pieces

2 tablespoons butter, divided

2 cups finely chopped yellow onions

2 cups milk, divided

¾ teaspoon salt

¾ teaspoon curry powder

Pinch ground red pepper

1 Bring water to a boil in large saucepan over high heat. Add sweet potatoes; return to a boil. Reduce heat to medium-low; simmer 15 minutes or until sweet potatoes are tender.

2 Meanwhile, heat 1 tablespoon butter in medium skillet over medium-high heat. Add onions; cook 8 minutes or until tender and golden brown, stirring occasionally.

3 Drain sweet potatoes; transfer to blender. Add onions, 1 cup milk, salt, curry powder and red pepper to blender; blend until completely smooth.

4 Return sweet potato mixture to saucepan. Stir in remaining 1 cup milk; cook over medium-high heat 5 minutes or until heated through. Remove from heat; stir in remaining 1 tablespoon butter.

ROMAN SPINACH SOUP

Makes 8 servings

6 cups chicken broth

4 eggs

¼ cup minced fresh basil

¼ cup grated Parmesan cheese

2 tablespoons lemon juice

1 tablespoon minced fresh parsley

¼ teaspoon white pepper

⅛ teaspoon ground nutmeg

8 cups packed fresh spinach, stemmed and chopped

1 Bring broth to a boil in large saucepan over medium heat.

2 Whisk eggs, basil, cheese, lemon juice, parsley, pepper and nutmeg in small bowl until well blended.

3 Add spinach to broth; cook and stir 1 minute. Slowly pour egg mixture into broth, whisking constantly so egg threads form. Cook 2 to 3 minutes or until egg is cooked. Serve immediately.

Note

Soup may look curdled.

TWO-CHEESE POTATO AND CAULIFLOWER SOUP

Makes 4 to 6 servings

1 tablespoon butter

1 cup chopped onion

2 cloves garlic, minced

5 cups whole milk

1 pound Yukon Gold potatoes, peeled and diced

1 pound cauliflower florets

1½ teaspoons salt

⅛ teaspoon ground red pepper

1½ cups (6 ounces) shredded sharp Cheddar cheese

⅓ cup crumbled blue cheese

1 Melt butter in large saucepan over medium-high heat. Add onion; cook and stir 4 minutes or until translucent. Add garlic; cook and stir 15 seconds.

2 Stir in milk, potatoes, cauliflower, salt and red pepper; bring to a boil. Reduce heat to low; cover and simmer 15 minutes or until potatoes are tender. Cool slightly.

3 Blend soup with hand-held immersion blender until smooth. (Or blend soup in batches in blender or food processor.) Cook and stir over medium heat just until heated through. Remove from heat; stir in cheeses until melted.

Tip

One pound of trimmed cauliflower will yield about 1½ cups of florets. You can also substitute 1 pound of frozen cauliflower florets for the fresh florets.

SIMPLE SKILLET VEGETABLE BEAN SOUP
Makes 4 servings

2 tablespoons olive oil, divided

1 medium orange, red or yellow bell pepper, chopped

1 clove garlic, minced

2 cups water

1 can (about 14 ounces) diced tomatoes

1 medium zucchini, thinly sliced lengthwise

¾ teaspoon salt

⅛ teaspoon red pepper flakes

1 can (about 15 ounces) navy beans, rinsed and drained

3 to 4 tablespoons chopped fresh basil

1 tablespoon balsamic vinegar

½ teaspoon liquid smoke (optional)

1 Heat 1 tablespoon oil in large skillet over medium-high heat. Add bell pepper; cook and stir 4 minutes or until edges are browned. Add garlic; cook and stir 15 seconds.

2 Stir in water, tomatoes, zucchini, salt and red pepper flakes; bring to a boil over high heat. Reduce heat to low; cover and simmer 20 minutes.

3 Stir in beans, basil, remaining 1 tablespoon oil, vinegar and liquid smoke, if desired; cook 5 minutes. Remove from heat; cover and let stand 5 minutes before serving.

ITALIAN MUSHROOM SOUP
Makes 6 to 8 servings

½ cup dried porcini mushrooms (about ½ ounce)

1 tablespoon olive oil

2 cups chopped onions

8 ounces sliced cremini or button mushrooms

2 cloves garlic, minced

¼ teaspoon dried thyme

¼ cup all-purpose flour

4 cups vegetable broth

½ teaspoon salt

½ cup whipping cream

⅓ cup Marsala wine (optional)

Black pepper

1 Place dried mushrooms in small bowl; cover with boiling water. Let stand 15 minutes or until softened.

2 Meanwhile, heat oil in large saucepan over medium heat. Add onions; cook 5 minutes or until translucent, stirring occasionally. Add cremini mushrooms, garlic and thyme; cook 8 minutes, stirring occasionally. If desired, set aside a few sautéed mushrooms for garnish. Add flour to saucepan; cook and stir 1 minute. Stir in broth and salt.

3 Drain porcini mushrooms, reserving liquid. Chop mushrooms; add to saucepan with reserved soaking liquid. Bring to a boil over medium-high heat. Reduce heat to medium-low; simmer 10 minutes. Cool slightly.

4 Blend soup with hand-held immersion blender until smooth. (Or blend soup in batches in blender or food processor.) Stir in cream and Marsala, if desired; cook over medium-low heat 5 minutes or until heated through. Season with additional salt and pepper; garnish with reserved mushrooms.

CREAM OF BROCCOLI SOUP WITH CROUTONS
Makes 8 servings

3 cups French or rustic country bread, cut into ½-inch cubes

1 tablespoon butter, melted

1 tablespoon olive oil

¼ cup grated Parmesan cheese

2 tablespoons butter

1 large onion, chopped

8 cups (about 1½ pounds) chopped broccoli

3 cups chicken broth

1 cup whipping cream or half-and-half

1½ teaspoons salt

½ teaspoon black pepper

1 Preheat oven to 350°F. Combine bread cubes, 1 tablespoon melted butter and oil in large bowl; toss to coat. Add cheese; toss again. Spread bread cubes on large rimmed baking sheet.

2 Bake 12 to 14 minutes or until golden brown, stirring after 8 minutes. Cool completely. (Croutons may be prepared up to 2 days before serving; store in airtight container.)

3 Heat 2 tablespoons butter in large saucepan or Dutch oven over medium heat. Add onion; cook 5 minutes, stirring occasionally. Stir in broccoli and broth; bring to a boil over high heat. Reduce heat to low; simmer 25 minutes or until broccoli is very tender. Cool 10 minutes.

4 Blend soup with hand-held immersion blender until smooth. (Or blend soup in batches in blender or food processor.) Stir in cream, salt and pepper; cook over medium heat until heated through. (Do not boil.) Top with croutons.

CURRIED GINGER PUMPKIN SOUP

Makes 8 servings

1 tablespoon vegetable oil

1 large sweet onion
   (such as Walla Walla),
   coarsely chopped

1 large Golden Delicious
   apple, peeled and
   coarsely chopped

3 (¼-inch) slices peeled
   fresh ginger

1½ teaspoons curry powder

2½ to 3 cups chicken broth,
   divided

2 cans (15 ounces each)
   pure pumpkin

1 cup half-and-half

1 teaspoon salt

   Black pepper

   Roasted salted pumpkin
   seeds (optional)

1 Heat oil in large saucepan or Dutch oven over medium heat. Add onion, apple, ginger and curry powder; cook 10 minutes, stirring occasionally. Add ½ cup broth; cover and simmer 10 minutes or until apple is tender.

2 Blend onion mixture with hand-held immersion blender until smooth. (Or transfer to blender; blend until smooth and return to saucepan.)

3 Stir in pumpkin, 2 cups broth, half-and-half, salt and pepper; cook over medium heat about 5 minutes or until heated through, stirring occasionally. If soup is too thick, add additional broth, a few tablespoons at a time, until soup reaches desired consistency. Garnish with pumpkin seeds.

RIBOLLITA (TUSCAN BREAD SOUP)
Makes 6 servings

2 tablespoons olive oil

1 onion, halved and thinly sliced

2 stalks celery, diced

1 large carrot, julienned

2 medium zucchini, halved lengthwise and thinly sliced

1 medium yellow squash, halved lengthwise and thinly sliced

3 cloves garlic, minced

1 can (about 28 ounces) whole tomatoes, undrained, coarsely chopped

1 can (15 ounces) cannellini beans, rinsed and drained

1½ teaspoons salt

1 teaspoon Italian seasoning

¼ teaspoon black pepper

1 bay leaf

¼ teaspoon red pepper flakes (optional)

4 cups vegetable broth

2 cups water

1 bunch kale, stemmed and coarsely chopped *or* 3 cups thinly sliced cabbage

8 ounces Tuscan or other rustic bread, cubed

Shredded Parmesan cheese (optional)

1 Heat oil in large saucepan or Dutch oven over medium-high heat. Add onion, celery and carrot; cook and stir 5 minutes. Add zucchini, yellow squash and garlic; cook and stir 5 minutes.

2 Add tomatoes, beans, salt, Italian seasoning, black pepper, bay leaf and red pepper flakes, if desired. Stir in broth and water; bring to a boil. Reduce heat to low; simmer 15 minutes.

3 Add kale and bread; cook 10 minutes or until vegetables are tender, bread is soft and soup is thick. Serve with cheese, if desired.

Note

This recipe is a great way to use up stale or day-old bread. Cut the bread in cubes ahead of time and leave it out at room temperature for several hours. Or spread the bread cubes on a baking sheet and bake at 350°F until bread is dry but not browned.

GROUNDNUT SOUP WITH GINGER AND CILANTRO
Makes 4 servings

1 tablespoon vegetable oil

1½ cups chopped onion

1 clove garlic, minced

2 teaspoons chili powder

1 teaspoon ground cumin

¼ teaspoon red pepper flakes

3 cups vegetable broth

1 can (about 14 ounces) diced tomatoes

8 ounces sweet potatoes, peeled and cut into ½-inch pieces

1 medium carrot, cut into ½-inch pieces

¼ teaspoon salt

1 cup salted peanuts

1 tablespoon grated fresh ginger

¼ cup chopped fresh cilantro

1 Heat oil in large saucepan or Dutch oven over medium-high heat. Add onion; cook and stir 4 minutes or until translucent. Add garlic, chili powder, cumin and red pepper flakes; cook and stir 15 seconds.

2 Stir in broth, tomatoes, sweet potatoes, carrot and salt; bring to a boil over high heat. Reduce heat to medium; cover and simmer 25 minutes or until vegetables are tender, stirring occasionally. Remove from heat; stir in peanuts and ginger. Cool slightly.

3 Blend soup with hand-held immersion blender until smooth. (Or blend soup in batches in blender or food processor.) Cook over medium-high heat 2 minutes or until heated through. Sprinkle with cilantro.

PASTA
and
NOODLE
SOUPS

SAUSAGE VEGETABLE ROTINI SOUP
Makes 4 servings

1 tablespoon olive oil

6 ounces bulk pork sausage

1 cup chopped onion

1 cup chopped green
   bell pepper

3 cups beef broth

1 can (about 14 ounces)
   diced tomatoes

¼ cup ketchup

2 teaspoons chili powder

¼ teaspoon salt

4 ounces uncooked
   tri-colored rotini pasta

1 cup frozen corn, thawed
   and drained

1 Heat oil in large saucepan over medium-high heat. Add sausage; cook 3 minutes or until no longer pink, stirring to break up meat. Drain fat. Add onion and bell pepper; cook and stir 3 to 4 minutes or until onion is translucent.

2 Stir in broth, tomatoes, ketchup, chili powder and salt; bring to a boil over high heat. Stir in pasta; return to a boil. Reduce heat to medium-low; simmer 12 minutes.

3 Stir in corn; cook 2 minutes or until pasta is tender and corn is heated through.

PEPPERY SICILIAN CHICKEN SOUP
Makes 8 to 10 servings

2 tablespoons olive oil

1 onion, chopped

1 green bell pepper, chopped

3 stalks celery, chopped

3 carrots, chopped

3 cloves garlic, minced

1 tablespoon salt

3 containers (32 ounces each) chicken broth

2 pounds boneless skinless chicken breasts

1 can (28 ounces) diced tomatoes

2 baking potatoes, peeled and cut into ¼-inch pieces

1½ teaspoons ground white pepper*

1½ teaspoons ground black pepper

½ cup chopped fresh parsley

8 ounces uncooked ditalini pasta

Or substitute additional black pepper for the white pepper.

1 Heat oil in large saucepan or Dutch oven over medium heat. Stir in onion, bell pepper, celery and carrots. Reduce heat to medium-low; cover and cook 10 to 15 minutes or until vegetables are tender but not browned, stirring occasionally. Stir in garlic and 1 tablespoon salt; cover and cook 5 minutes.

2 Stir in broth, chicken, tomatoes, potatoes, white pepper and black pepper; bring to a boil. Reduce heat to low; cover and simmer 1 hour.

3 Remove chicken to plate; set aside until cool enough to handle. Shred chicken and return to saucepan with parsley.

4 Meanwhile, cook pasta in medium saucepan of boiling salted water 7 minutes (or 1 minute less than package directs for al dente). Drain pasta and add to soup. Taste and season with additional salt, if desired.

JAPANESE NOODLE SOUP
Makes 4 to 6 servings

1 package (8½ ounces) Japanese udon noodles

1 tablespoon vegetable oil

1 medium red bell pepper, cut into thin strips

1 medium carrot, diagonally sliced

2 green onions, thinly sliced

2 cans (about 14 ounces each) beef broth

1 cup water

1 teaspoon soy sauce

½ teaspoon grated fresh ginger

½ teaspoon black pepper

2 cups thinly sliced fresh shiitake mushrooms, stems discarded

4 ounces daikon (Japanese radish), peeled and cut into thin strips

4 ounces firm tofu, drained and cut into ½-inch cubes

1 Cook noodles according to package directions. Drain and rinse noodles; set aside.

2 Heat oil in large saucepan over medium-high heat. Add bell pepper, carrot and green onions; cook and stir 3 minutes or until vegetables are slightly softened.

3 Stir in broth, water, soy sauce, ginger and black pepper; bring to a boil. Stir in mushrooms, daikon and tofu. Reduce heat to low; simmer 5 minutes.

4 Place noodles in serving bowls; ladle soup over noodles.

ITALIAN WEDDING SOUP
Makes 8 servings

MEATBALLS

- 2 eggs
- 2 cloves garlic, minced
- 1 teaspoon salt
- ⅛ teaspoon black pepper
- 1½ pounds meat loaf mix (ground beef and pork)
- ¾ cup plain dry bread crumbs
- ½ cup grated Parmesan cheese
- 2 tablespoons olive oil

SOUP

- 1 onion, chopped
- 2 carrots, chopped
- 4 cloves garlic, minced
- 2 heads escarole or curly endive, coarsely chopped
- 8 cups chicken broth
- 1 can (about 14 ounces) Italian plum tomatoes, undrained, coarsely chopped
- 3 sprigs fresh thyme
- 1 teaspoon salt
- ½ teaspoon red pepper flakes
- 1 cup uncooked acini di pepe pasta

1 For meatballs, beat eggs, 2 cloves garlic, 1 teaspoon salt and black pepper in large bowl until blended. Stir in meat loaf mix, bread crumbs and cheese; mix gently until well blended. Shape tablespoonfuls of mixture into 1-inch balls.

2 Heat oil in large saucepan or Dutch oven over medium heat. Cook meatballs in batches 5 minutes or until browned. Remove to plate; set aside.

3 For soup, add onion, carrots and 4 cloves garlic to same saucepan; cook and stir 5 minutes or until onion is lightly browned. Add escarole; cook and stir 2 minutes or until wilted. Stir in broth, tomatoes with juice, thyme, 1 teaspoon salt and red pepper flakes; bring to a boil over high heat. Reduce heat to medium-low; simmer 15 minutes.

4 Add meatballs and pasta to soup; return to a boil over high heat. Reduce heat to medium; cook 10 minutes or until pasta is tender. Remove and discard thyme sprigs before serving.

PESTO TORTELLINI SOUP
Makes 6 servings

1 package (9 ounces) refrigerated cheese tortellini

3 cans (about 14 ounces each) chicken or vegetable broth

1 jar (7 ounces) roasted red peppers, drained and thinly sliced

¾ cup frozen green peas

3 to 4 cups packed stemmed fresh spinach

1 to 2 tablespoons pesto sauce

Grated Parmesan cheese (optional)

1 Cook tortellini according to package directions; drain.

2 Heat broth to a boil in large saucepan or Dutch oven over high heat. Add cooked tortellini, roasted peppers and peas; return to a boil. Reduce heat to medium; cook 1 minute.

3 Remove from heat; stir in spinach and pesto. Serve with cheese, if desired.

VEGETABLE BEEF NOODLE SOUP
Makes 4 servings

1 tablespoon olive oil

8 ounces beef stew meat
   (½-inch pieces)

¾ cup unpeeled cubed
   potato (1 medium)

½ cup sliced carrot

1 tablespoon balsamic
   vinegar

¾ teaspoon dried thyme

½ teaspoon salt

¼ teaspoon black pepper

2½ cups beef broth

1 cup water

¼ cup chili sauce or ketchup

2 ounces uncooked thin
   egg noodles

¾ cup jarred or canned
   pearl onions, rinsed
   and drained

¼ cup frozen peas

1 Heat oil in large saucepan over medium-high heat. Add beef; cook about 3 minutes or until browned on all sides, stirring occasionally. Remove to plate.

2 Add potato, carrot, vinegar, thyme, salt and pepper to saucepan; cook and stir 3 minutes. Stir in broth, water and chili sauce; bring to a boil.

3 Stir in beef. Reduce heat to medium-low; cover and simmer 30 minutes or until meat is almost fork-tender.

4 Bring soup to a boil over medium-high heat. Add noodles; cover and cook 7 to 10 minutes or until noodles are tender, stirring occasionally. Add onions and peas; cook 1 minute or until heated through. Serve immediately.

FENNEL PASTA SOUP
Makes 6 servings

1 tablespoon olive oil

1 small fennel bulb, trimmed and chopped into ¼-inch pieces (1½ cups)

4 cloves garlic, minced

3 cups vegetable broth

1 cup uncooked small shell pasta

1 medium zucchini or yellow squash, cut into ½-inch pieces

1 can (about 14 ounces) Italian-style diced tomatoes

¼ cup grated Romano or Parmesan cheese

¼ cup chopped fresh basil

Pinch black pepper

1 Heat oil in large saucepan over medium heat. Add fennel; cook and stir 5 minutes. Add garlic; cook and stir 30 seconds. Stir in broth and pasta; bring to a boil over high heat. Reduce heat to low; simmer 5 minutes.

2 Add zucchini; cook 5 to 7 minutes or until pasta and vegetables are tender, stirring occasionally.

3 Stir in tomatoes; cook until heated through. Top with cheese, basil and pepper.

CHICKEN AND HOMEMADE NOODLE SOUP

Makes 4 servings

¾ cup all-purpose flour

2 teaspoons finely chopped fresh thyme *or* ½ teaspoon dried thyme, divided

¼ teaspoon salt

1 egg yolk, beaten

2 cups plus 3 tablespoons cold water, divided

1 pound boneless skinless chicken thighs, cut into ½- to ¾-inch pieces

5 cups chicken broth

1 onion, chopped

1 carrot, thinly sliced

¾ cup frozen peas

Chopped fresh Italian parsley

1 Combine flour, 1 teaspoon thyme and salt in small bowl. Stir in egg yolk and 3 tablespoons water until well blended. Shape dough into a ball.

2 Place dough on lightly floured surface; flatten slightly. Knead 5 minutes or until dough is smooth and elastic, adding additional flour to prevent sticking, if necessary. Cover with plastic wrap; let stand 15 minutes.

3 Roll out dough to ⅛-inch thickness or thinner on lightly floured surface. If dough is too elastic, let rest several minutes. Let dough rest about 30 minutes to dry slightly. Cut dough into ¼-inch-wide strips; cut strips 1½ to 2 inches long.

4 Combine chicken and remaining 2 cups water in medium saucepan; bring to a boil over high heat. Reduce heat to medium-low; cover and simmer 5 minutes or until chicken is cooked through. Drain chicken; set aside.

5 Combine broth, onion, carrot and remaining 1 teaspoon thyme in large saucepan or Dutch oven; bring to a boil over high heat. Add noodles. Reduce heat to medium-low; cook 8 minutes or until noodles are tender. Stir in chicken and peas; cook just until heated through. Sprinkle with parsley.

BEEF GOULASH SOUP
Makes 8 servings

1 tablespoon vegetable oil

1¼ pounds boneless beef sirloin tri-tip roast,* cut into 1-inch pieces

1 cup chopped onion

3 cans (about 14 ounces each) beef broth

2 cans (about 14 ounces each) diced tomatoes

1½ cups sliced carrots

2 tablespoons sugar

1 tablespoon paprika

1 tablespoon caraway seeds, slightly crushed

2 cloves garlic, minced

1 teaspoon salt

4 ounces (about 2 cups) uncooked whole wheat noodles

2 cups thinly sliced cabbage or coleslaw mix

Or substitute chuck roast or beef round steak.

1 Heat oil in large saucepan or Dutch oven over medium heat. Cook beef in two batches until browned; remove to plate.

2 Add onion to saucepan; cook and stir 3 minutes or until tender.

3 Return beef to saucepan. Stir in broth, tomatoes, carrots, sugar, paprika, caraway seeds, garlic and salt; bring to a boil. Reduce heat to medium-low; cover and simmer 45 minutes or until beef is tender.

4 Stir in noodles; bring to a boil. Reduce heat to medium-low; cook, uncovered, 10 minutes or until noodles are tender. Stir in cabbage; cook 2 minutes or until heated through.

LONG SOUP
Makes 4 servings

1 tablespoon vegetable oil

8 ounces boneless pork loin, cut into thin strips

¼ small head green cabbage, shredded

6 cups chicken broth

2 tablespoons soy sauce

½ teaspoon minced fresh ginger

8 green onions, cut diagonally into ½-inch slices

4 ounces uncooked Chinese-style thin egg noodles

1 Heat oil in large saucepan over medium-high heat. Add pork and cabbage; cook and stir about 5 minutes or until pork is no longer pink in center.

2 Add broth, soy sauce and ginger; bring to a boil. Reduce heat to low; simmer 10 minutes, stirring occasionally. Stir in green onions.

3 Stir in noodles; cook 2 to 4 minutes or until noodles are tender.

CHICKEN VEGETABLE SOUP
Makes 4 servings

2 tablespoons butter

8 ounces boneless skinless chicken breasts, cut into ½-inch pieces

½ medium onion, chopped

4 ounces mushrooms, sliced

4 cups chicken broth

2 teaspoons Worcestershire sauce

¼ teaspoon salt

¼ teaspoon dried tarragon

¾ cup uncooked rotini pasta

1 small zucchini, cut crosswise into ⅛-inch slices

1 Melt butter in large saucepan over medium heat. Add chicken, onion and mushrooms; cook and stir 5 minutes or until onion is softened and chicken is lightly browned.

2 Stir in broth, Worcestershire sauce, salt and tarragon; bring to a boil over high heat. Stir in pasta. Reduce heat to medium-low; cook 5 minutes, stirring occasionally.

3 Add zucchini to soup; cook about 5 minutes or until pasta is tender.

PASTA AND BEAN SOUP
Makes 6 servings

1¼ cups dried navy beans

6 cups cold water

3 slices bacon, finely chopped

1 onion, chopped

1 stalk celery, chopped

12 ounces smoked pork rib or neck bones or ham hocks

2 cloves garlic, minced

½ teaspoon dried thyme

½ teaspoon dried marjoram

¼ teaspoon black pepper

¾ cup uncooked small pasta shells

2 tablespoons chopped fresh parsley

Salt

1 cup beef broth (optional)

Grated Parmesan cheese

1 Rinse beans in colander under cold water, removing any debris or blemished beans. Combine beans and water in large saucepan or Dutch oven. To quick soak beans, bring to a boil over high heat; boil 2 minutes. Remove from heat; cover and let stand 1 hour. Do not drain.

2 Cook bacon in medium skillet over medium-high heat 2 minutes. Add onion and celery; cook and stir 6 minutes or until golden brown. Remove bacon, onion and celery to plate; drain off drippings.

3 Rinse pork bones; add to saucepan with beans and soaking water. Stir in bacon mixture, garlic, thyme, marjoram and pepper; bring to a boil over high heat. Reduce heat to medium-low; simmer 1 hour or until beans are tender, stirring occasionally. Remove from heat.

4 Remove pork bones to plate; set aside to cool. Transfer half of bean mixture to food processor or blender with slotted spoon. Add 2 tablespoons liquid from soup; process until smooth.

5 Stir puréed bean mixture back into soup; bring to a boil over high heat. Stir in pasta. Reduce heat to medium-low; cook 10 minutes or until pasta is tender, stirring occasionally.

6 Meanwhile, remove meat from pork bones; discard bones. Chop pork into bite-size pieces. Stir pork and parsley into soup; season with salt. If soup is too thick, add broth until desired consistency is reached. Sprinkle with cheese.

TURKEY NOODLE SOUP
Makes about 6 servings

3 pounds turkey thighs, wings and necks

8 cups water

5 carrots, coarsely chopped, divided

1 small onion, quartered

1 teaspoon salt

¼ teaspoon dried thyme

¼ teaspoon dried sage leaves

1 can (about 14 ounces) chicken broth

6 ounces uncooked egg noodles

Finely chopped fresh parsley

1 Place turkey in Dutch oven. Add water, 2 carrots, onion, salt, thyme and sage; bring to a boil over high heat. Reduce heat to medium-low; cover and simmer 1 hour.

2 Stir in broth; simmer, uncovered, 30 minutes or until turkey is fork-tender.

3 Remove turkey and vegetables from broth; discard vegetables. Remove meat from bones; discard skin and bones. Cut turkey into bite-size pieces.

4 Return broth to a boil over medium heat. Add turkey, remaining 3 carrots and noodles; cook, uncovered, 10 minutes or until noodles are tender. Adjust seasoning, if desired. Stir in parsley.

PASTA MEATBALL SOUP
Makes 4 servings

10 ounces ground beef

5 tablespoons uncooked acini di pepe pasta,* divided

¼ cup fresh fine bread crumbs

1 egg

2 tablespoons finely chopped fresh parsley, divided

1 teaspoon dried basil, divided

1 clove garlic, minced

½ teaspoon salt

⅛ teaspoon black pepper

2 cans (about 14 ounces each) beef broth

1 can (8 ounces) tomato sauce

⅓ cup chopped onion

Acini di pepe is tiny rice-shaped pasta. Orzo or pastina can be substituted.

1 Combine beef, 2 tablespoons pasta, bread crumbs, egg, 1 tablespoon parsley, ½ teaspoon basil, garlic, salt and pepper in medium bowl; mix gently. Shape into 28 to 30 (1-inch) meatballs.

2 Combine broth, tomato sauce, onion and remaining ½ teaspoon basil in large saucepan; bring to a boil over medium-high heat. Carefully add meatballs to broth mixture. Reduce heat to medium-low; cover and simmer 20 minutes.

3 Add remaining 3 tablespoons pasta to saucepan; cook, uncovered, 10 minutes or until tender, stirring occasionally. Sprinkle with remaining 1 tablespoon parsley.

BEAN and GRAIN SOUPS

FASOLADA (GREEK WHITE BEAN SOUP)
Makes 4 to 6 servings

4 tablespoons olive oil, divided

1 large onion, diced

3 stalks celery, diced

3 carrots, diced

4 cloves garlic, minced

¼ cup tomato paste

1 teaspoon salt

1 teaspoon dried oregano

½ teaspoon ground cumin

¼ teaspoon black pepper

1 bay leaf

4 cups vegetable broth

3 cans (15 ounces each) cannellini beans, rinsed and drained

2 tablespoons lemon juice

¼ cup minced fresh parsley

1 Heat 2 tablespoons oil in large saucepan over medium-high heat. Add onion, celery and carrots; cook and stir 8 to 10 minutes or until vegetables are softened. Add garlic; cook and stir 30 seconds. Stir in tomato paste, salt, oregano, cumin, pepper and bay leaf; cook and stir 30 seconds.

2 Stir in broth; bring to a boil. Stir in beans; return to a boil. Reduce heat to medium-low; simmer 30 minutes.

3 Stir in remaining 2 tablespoons oil and lemon juice. Remove and discard bay leaf. Sprinkle with parsley just before serving.

SAUSAGE RICE SOUP
Makes 4 to 6 servings

2 teaspoons olive oil

8 ounces Italian sausage, casings removed

1 small onion, chopped

½ teaspoon fennel seeds

1 tablespoon tomato paste

4 cups chicken broth

1 can (about 14 ounces) whole tomatoes, undrained, crushed with hands or coarsely chopped

1½ cups water

½ cup uncooked rice

¼ teaspoon salt

⅛ teaspoon black pepper

2 to 3 ounces baby spinach

⅓ cup shredded mozzarella cheese (optional)

1 Heat oil in large saucepan or Dutch oven over medium-high heat. Add sausage; cook 8 minutes or until browned, stirring to break up meat. Add onion; cook and stir 5 minutes or until softened. Add fennel seeds; cook and stir 30 seconds. Add tomato paste; cook and stir 1 minute.

2 Stir in broth, tomatoes with juice, water, rice, ¼ teaspoon salt and ⅛ teaspoon pepper; bring to a boil. Reduce heat to medium-low; simmer 18 minutes or until rice is tender.

3 Stir in spinach; cook 3 minutes or until wilted. Season with additional salt and pepper.

4 Sprinkle with cheese, if desired, just before serving.

COUNTRY BEAN SOUP
Makes 6 servings

1¼ cups dried navy beans
    or lima beans, rinsed
    and sorted

2½ cups water

4 ounces ham or salt pork,
    chopped

¼ cup chopped onion

½ teaspoon dried oregano

¼ teaspoon salt

¼ teaspoon ground ginger

¼ teaspoon dried sage

¼ teaspoon black pepper

2 cups milk

2 tablespoons butter

1 Place beans in large saucepan; add water to cover. Bring to a boil over medium-high heat. Reduce heat to medium-low; cook 2 minutes. Remove from heat; cover and let stand 1 hour.

2 Drain beans and return to saucepan. Stir in 2½ cups water, ham, onion, oregano, salt, ginger, sage and pepper; bring to a boil over high heat. Reduce heat to medium-low; cover and simmer 2 hours or until beans are tender. (If necessary, add additional water to keep beans covered during cooking.)

3 Add milk and butter; cook and stir until heated through.

LENTIL SOUP
Makes 6 to 8 servings

- 2 tablespoons olive oil, divided
- 2 medium onions, chopped
- 1½ teaspoons salt
- 4 cloves garlic, minced
- ¼ cup tomato paste
- 1 teaspoon dried oregano
- ½ teaspoon dried basil
- ¼ teaspoon dried thyme
- ¼ teaspoon black pepper
- ½ cup dry sherry or white wine
- 8 cups vegetable broth
- 2 cups water
- 3 carrots, cut into ½-inch pieces
- 2 cups dried lentils, rinsed and sorted
- 1 cup chopped fresh parsley
- 1 tablespoon balsamic vinegar

1 Heat 1 tablespoon oil in large saucepan or Dutch oven over medium heat. Add onions; cook 10 minutes, stirring occasionally. Add remaining 1 tablespoon oil and salt; cook 10 minutes or until onions are golden brown, stirring frequently.

2 Add garlic; cook and stir 1 minute. Add tomato paste, oregano, basil, thyme and pepper; cook and stir 1 minute. Stir in sherry; cook 30 seconds, scraping up browned bits from bottom of saucepan.

3 Stir in broth, water, carrots and lentils; cover and bring to a boil over high heat. Reduce heat to medium-low; cook, partially covered, 30 minutes or until lentils are tender.

4 Remove from heat; stir in parsley and vinegar.

BLACK BEAN SOUP
Makes 4 to 6 servings

2 tablespoons vegetable oil

1 cup diced onion

1 stalk celery, diced

2 carrots, diced

½ small green bell pepper, diced

4 cloves garlic, minced

4 cans (about 15 ounces each) black beans, rinsed and drained, divided

4 cups chicken or vegetable broth, divided

2 tablespoons cider vinegar

2 teaspoons chili powder

½ teaspoon salt

½ teaspoon ground red pepper

½ teaspoon ground cumin

¼ teaspoon liquid smoke

Optional toppings: sour cream, chopped green onions and/or shredded Cheddar cheese

1 Heat oil in large saucepan or Dutch oven over medium-low heat. Add onion, celery, carrots, bell pepper and garlic; cook 10 minutes, stirring occasionally.

2 Combine half of beans and 1 cup broth in food processor or blender; process until smooth. Add to vegetables in saucepan.

3 Stir in remaining beans, 3 cups broth, vinegar, chili powder, salt, red pepper, cumin and liquid smoke; bring to a boil over high heat. Reduce heat to medium-low; simmer 1 hour or until vegetables are tender and soup is thickened, stirring occasionally. Garnish as desired.

TURKEY VEGETABLE RICE SOUP
Makes 6 servings

1½ pounds turkey drumsticks
(2 small)

8 cups cold water

1 medium onion, cut
into quarters

2 tablespoons soy sauce

¼ teaspoon black pepper

1 bay leaf

2 carrots, sliced

⅓ cup uncooked rice

4 ounces mushrooms, sliced

1 cup fresh snow peas,
cut in half crosswise

1 cup coarsely chopped
bok choy

1 Place turkey in large saucepan or Dutch oven. Add water, onion, soy sauce, pepper and bay leaf; bring to a boil over high heat. Reduce heat to medium-low; simmer, uncovered, 1½ hours or until turkey is tender.

2 Remove turkey to plate; set aside until cool enough to handle. Let broth cool slightly; skim fat. Remove and discard bay leaf. Remove turkey meat from bones; discard skin and bones. Cut turkey into bite-size pieces.

3 Add carrots and rice to broth in saucepan; bring to a boil over high heat. Reduce heat to medium-low; simmer 10 minutes.

4 Add mushrooms and turkey to soup; bring to a boil over high heat. Reduce heat to medium-low; cook 5 minutes. Add snow peas and bok choy; bring to a boil over high heat. Reduce heat to medium-low; cook 8 minutes or until rice and vegetables are tender.

GREENS, BEANS AND BARLEY SOUP
Makes 8 servings

2 tablespoons olive oil

1½ cups chopped onions

3 carrots, diced

2 cloves garlic, minced

1½ cups sliced mushrooms

6 cups vegetable broth

2 cups cooked barley

1 can (about 15 ounces) Great Northern beans, rinsed and drained

2 bay leaves

1 teaspoon salt

1 teaspoon sugar

1 teaspoon dried thyme

7 cups chopped stemmed collard greens (about 24 ounces)

1 tablespoon white wine vinegar

Hot pepper sauce

Red bell pepper strips (optional)

1 Heat oil in large saucepan or Dutch oven over medium heat. Add onions, carrots and garlic; cook and stir 3 minutes. Add mushrooms; cook and stir 5 minutes or until carrots are tender.

2 Stir in broth, barley, beans, bay leaves, salt, sugar and thyme; bring to a boil over high heat. Reduce heat to medium-low; cover and simmer 5 minutes. Stir in greens; cook 10 minutes.

3 Remove and discard bay leaves. Stir in vinegar; season with hot pepper sauce. Garnish with red bell peppers.

SMOKY NAVY BEAN SOUP
Makes 6 servings

- 2 tablespoons olive oil, divided
- 4 ounces Canadian bacon or ham, diced
- 1 cup diced onion
- 1 carrot, thinly sliced
- 1 stalk celery, thinly sliced
- 3 cups water
- 6 ounces red potatoes, diced
- 2 bay leaves
- ¼ teaspoon dried tarragon
- 1 can (about 15 ounces) navy beans, rinsed and drained
- 1 teaspoon liquid smoke
- ½ teaspoon salt
- ½ teaspoon black pepper

1 Heat 1 tablespoon oil in large saucepan over medium-high heat. Add Canadian bacon; cook and stir 2 minutes or until browned. Remove to plate.

2 Add remaining 1 tablespoons oil, onion, carrot and celery to saucepan; cook and stir 4 minutes or until onion is translucent. Add water; bring to a boil. Stir in potatoes, bay leaves and tarragon. Reduce heat to medium-low; cover and simmer 20 minutes or until potatoes are tender.

3 Stir in beans, Canadian bacon, liquid smoke, salt and pepper; cook 5 minutes or until heated through. Remove and discard bay leaves.

FRENCH LENTIL RICE SOUP
Makes 4 servings

6 cups vegetable broth

1 cup dried lentils, rinsed and sorted

2 carrots, finely diced

1 onion, finely chopped

2 stalks celery, finely diced

3 tablespoons uncooked rice

2 teaspoons minced garlic

1 teaspoon herbes de Provence

½ teaspoon salt

⅛ teaspoon black pepper

4 tablespoons sour cream

¼ cup chopped fresh parsley

Slow Cooker Directions

1 Combine broth, lentils, carrots, onion, celery, rice, garlic, herbes de Provence, salt and pepper in slow cooker; mix well.

2 Cover; cook on LOW 8 hours or on HIGH 4 hours.

3 Transfer about 1½ cups soup to blender or food processor; blend until almost smooth. Return to slow cooker; stir until blended. Top each serving with cream and parsley.

HAM AND WHITE BEAN SOUP
Makes 8 servings

1 tablespoon olive oil

1 large onion, diced

3 carrots, chopped

2 stalks celery, chopped

4 cloves garlic, minced

1 teaspoon salt

1 teaspoon dried thyme

½ teaspoon ground cumin

½ teaspoon black pepper

¼ teaspoon ground
   red pepper

1 pound dried Great
   Northern or navy
   beans, soaked
   8 hours or overnight

8 cups water

1 meaty ham bone

2 bay leaves

8 ounces fresh spinach,
   stemmed and coarsely
   chopped

1 Heat oil in Dutch oven over medium-high heat. Add onion, carrots, celery and garlic; cook and stir 5 minutes or until vegetables are softened. Add salt, thyme, cumin, black pepper and red pepper; cook and stir 1 minute.

2 Drain beans; add to Dutch oven with water, ham bone and bay leaves. Bring to a boil. Reduce heat to low, cover with lid slightly ajar and simmer 1 hour or until beans are soft.*

3 Remove and discard bay leaves. Remove ham bone to plate; let stand until cool enough to handle. Add spinach to soup; cook about 5 minutes or until wilted, stirring occasionally.

4 Remove remaining meat from ham bone; cut into bite-size pieces. Stir ham into soup; season with additional salt and pepper.

Navy beans may take longer to cook than Great Northern beans; check for doneness at 1 hour and cook an additional 30 minutes or more as necessary.

CHICKEN, BARLEY AND VEGETABLE SOUP

Makes 6 servings

8 ounces boneless skinless chicken breasts, cut into ½-inch pieces

8 ounces boneless skinless chicken thighs, cut into ½-inch pieces

¾ teaspoon salt

¼ teaspoon black pepper

1 tablespoon olive oil

½ cup uncooked pearl barley

4 cans (about 14 ounces each) chicken broth

2 cups water

1 bay leaf

2 cups baby carrots

2 cups diced peeled potatoes

2 cups sliced mushrooms

2 cups frozen peas

3 tablespoons sour cream

1 tablespoon chopped fresh dill *or* 1 teaspoon dried dill weed

1 Sprinkle chicken with salt and pepper. Heat oil in large saucepan over medium-high heat. Add chicken; cook without stirring 2 minutes or until golden brown. Turn chicken; cook 2 minutes. Remove to plate.

2 Add barley to saucepan; cook and stir 1 to 2 minutes or until barley begins to brown, adding 1 tablespoon broth, if necessary, to prevent burning. Add remaining broth, water and bay leaf; bring to a boil. Reduce heat to low; cover and simmer 30 minutes.

3 Add chicken, carrots, potatoes and mushrooms to saucepan; cook 10 minutes or until vegetables are tender, stirring occasionally. Add peas; cook 2 minutes. Remove and discard bay leaf.

4 Top each serving with sour cream and dill; serve immediately.

PANTRY BEAN AND SPINACH SOUP

Makes 4 to 6 servings

2 slices bacon, chopped

½ cup diced onion

1 unpeeled new red potato, diced

2 cans (about 14 ounces each) vegetable broth

1 teaspoon minced garlic

¾ teaspoon salt

½ teaspoon dried oregano

2 bay leaves

1 can (about 14 ounces) sliced carrots, drained

1 can (about 13 ounces) spinach or kale, drained

1 can (about 15 ounces) cannellini beans, rinsed and drained

⅓ cup finely chopped sun-dried tomatoes packed in oil

1 tablespoon olive oil

¼ teaspoon black pepper

1 Cook bacon in large saucepan over medium heat until crisp.

2 Add onion and potato to saucepan; cook and stir 10 minutes or until onion is browned.

3 Stir in broth, garlic, salt, oregano and bay leaves; bring to a simmer. Cover and simmer 5 minutes or until potato is tender.

4 Add carrots, kale, beans and sun-dried tomatoes; cook 5 minutes. Remove and discard bay leaves. Stir in oil and pepper.

SPLIT PEA SOUP
Makes 6 servings

1 package (16 ounces) dried green or yellow split peas

7 cups water

1 pound smoked ham hocks *or* 4 ounces smoked sausage links, sliced and quartered

2 carrots, chopped

1 onion, chopped

¾ teaspoon salt

½ teaspoon dried basil

¼ teaspoon dried oregano

¼ teaspoon black pepper

1 Rinse split peas in colander under cold water; discard any debris or blemished peas.

2 Combine split peas, water, ham hocks, carrots, onion, salt, basil, oregano and pepper in large saucepan or Dutch oven; bring to a boil over high heat. Reduce heat to medium-low; simmer 1 hour 15 minutes or until split peas are tender, stirring occasionally. Stir frequently near end of cooking to prevent soup from scorching.

3 Remove ham hocks to cutting board; let stand until cool enough to handle. Remove ham from hocks; chop meat and discard bones.

4 Pour 3 cups soup into blender or food processor; blend until smooth. Return blended soup to saucepan; stir in ham. If soup is too thick, add water until desired consistency is reached. Cook just until heated through.

 Tip

When blending hot soup in a blender, remove the center cap and cover the hole with a towel; this allows steam to escape and prevents pressure from building which could blow the lid off. Fill the blender no more than half full, and always start blending at low speed. Gradually increase to high speed if necessary to reach the desired consistency.

BREADS

RUSTIC YEAST BREADS

SAVORY QUICK BREADS

SMALL BREADS

RUSTIC YEAST BREADS

FARMER-STYLE SOUR CREAM BREAD
Makes 1 loaf

1 cup sour cream

3 tablespoons water

2½ to 3 cups all-purpose flour, divided

1 package (¼ ounce) active dry yeast

2 tablespoons sugar

1½ teaspoons salt

¼ teaspoon baking soda

1 teaspoon vegetable oil

1 tablespoon sesame or poppy seeds

1 Combine sour cream and water in small saucepan; heat over low heat to 110° to 120°F.

2 Combine 2 cups flour, yeast, sugar, salt and baking soda in large bowl of stand mixer. Add sour cream mixture; mix with dough hook at low speed 3 minutes. Add remaining flour, ¼ cup at a time; mix 5 minutes or until dough is smooth and elastic.

3 Line baking sheet with parchment paper. Shape dough into a ball; place on prepared baking sheet. Flatten into 8-inch circle. Brush top with oil; sprinkle with sesame seeds. Cover and let rise in warm place 1 hour or until doubled in size. Preheat oven to 350°F.

4 Bake 22 to 27 minutes or until golden brown. Remove to wire rack to cool completely.

EASY PIZZA BREAD
Makes 1 loaf

1 loaf (1 pound) frozen bread dough, thawed according to package directions

⅓ cup plus 2 tablespoons pizza sauce, divided

1 cup (4 ounces) shredded mozzarella cheese

½ cup shredded Parmesan cheese

1 egg, beaten

1 Preheat oven to 350°F. Line 9×5-inch loaf pan with parchment paper or spray with nonstick cooking spray.

2 Roll out dough into 20×10-inch rectangle on lightly floured surface. Spread ⅓ cup pizza sauce evenly over dough, leaving ½-inch borders. Sprinkle with mozzarella and Parmesan.

3 Starting with long side, roll up dough jelly-roll style; pinch seam to seal. Cut roll in half lengthwise; turn halves cut sides up. Twist halves together, keeping filling facing up as much as possible.

4 Arrange dough in prepared pan, winding twisted dough back and forth in pan. Brush top of dough with egg. Fill in crevices and folds of dough with spoonfuls of remaining pizza sauce.

5 Bake about 40 minutes or until bread is golden brown and cooked through. (Cover loosely with foil if dough browns too quickly.) Cool in pan on wire rack 10 minutes. Serve warm.

RUSTIC WHITE BREAD
Makes 1 loaf

5 cups all-purpose flour

2 cups warm water
   (105° to 115°F)

1 tablespoon salt

1 package (¼ ounce) instant
   or active dry yeast

1 Combine flour and warm water in large bowl; stir to form shaggy dough. Cover with clean kitchen towel; let stand 30 minutes to hydrate flour.

2 Sprinkle salt and yeast over dough; squeeze and fold with hands to incorporate. Turn out dough onto lightly floured surface; knead 2 minutes, adding additional flour by teaspoonfuls if needed (dough will be sticky). Shape dough into a ball; return to bowl. Cover and let rise 2 hours.

3 Gently fold edges of dough to center, pressing down lightly to form a ball. Turn dough over; cover and let rise 3 to 4 hours or until dough has large air bubbles.

4 Turn oven to 450°F; place 5- to 6-quart Dutch oven with lid in oven. Preheat oven and pot 30 minutes. Meanwhile, gently ease dough from bowl onto work surface with lightly floured hands, trying not to tear dough as much as possible (do not punch down dough). Wrap your hands around sides of dough and gently pull it across work surface to form a ball. Repeat until dough is a smooth ball. Lightly dust medium bowl with flour; place dough in bowl. Cover and let rise while oven and pot are heating.

5 Use oven mitts to carefully remove Dutch oven from oven and remove lid (pot and lid will be very hot). Gently turn out dough onto work surface; place in Dutch oven, bottom side up. Replace lid using oven mitts; return Dutch oven to oven.

6 Bake bread, covered, 30 minutes. Carefully remove lid; bake 10 to 12 minutes or until top is deep golden brown. Remove to wire rack to cool completely.

GANNAT (FRENCH CHEESE BREAD)
Makes 1 loaf

1 package (¼ ounce) active dry yeast

1 teaspoon sugar

4 to 6 tablespoons warm water (105° to 115°F)

2½ cups all-purpose flour

¼ cup (½ stick) butter, at room temperature

1 teaspoon salt

2 eggs

4 ounces Emmentaler Swiss, Gruyère, sharp Cheddar or Swiss cheese, shredded

1 teaspoon vegetable oil

1 Dissolve yeast and sugar in 4 tablespoons warm water in small bowl; let stand 5 minutes or until bubbly.

2 Combine flour, butter and salt in food processor; process 15 seconds or until blended. Add yeast mixture and eggs; process 15 seconds or just until blended.

3 With motor running, slowly drizzle just enough water through feed tube so dough forms a ball that cleans side of bowl. Process until ball turns around bowl about 25 times. Let dough rest 1 to 2 minutes. With motor running, drizzle in enough remaining water to make dough soft, smooth and satiny. Process until dough turns around bowl about 15 times.

4 Turn out dough onto lightly floured surface; shape into a ball. Place dough in greased bowl; turn to grease top. Cover and let rise in warm place about 1 hour or until doubled in size.

5 Spray 9-inch round cake pan or pie plate with nonstick cooking spray. Punch down dough. Place dough on lightly greased surface; knead cheese into dough. Roll or pat into 8-inch circle; brush with oil. Let rise in warm place about 45 minutes or until doubled in size. Preheat oven to 375°F.

6 Bake 30 to 35 minutes or until top is browned and bread sounds hollow when tapped. Remove to wire rack to cool completely.

QUICK WHITE CASSEROLE BREAD
Makes 1 loaf

2¾ cups all-purpose flour

3 tablespoons nonfat
   dry milk powder

1 package (¼ ounce)
   instant yeast

2 tablespoons sugar

1 teaspoon salt

1 cup warm water (120°F)

2 tablespoons vegetable oil

1 tablespoon sesame or
   poppy seeds (optional)

1 Combine flour, milk powder, yeast, sugar and salt in large bowl of stand mixer; mix with dough hook at low speed 1 minute. With mixer running, add water and oil; mix at low speed 5 minutes.

2 Spray 1½-quart round baking dish with nonstick cooking spray. Scrape batter into prepared baking dish; smooth top and sprinkle with sesame seeds, if desired. Cover and let rise in warm place 45 minutes or until almost doubled in size. Preheat oven to 375°F.

3 Bake 25 to 30 minutes or until wooden skewer inserted into center comes out clean (190° to 200°F on instant-read thermometer). Cool in baking dish 10 minutes; remove to wire rack to cool completely.

Casserole Cheese Bread

Prepare batter as directed for Quick Casserole Bread. Pour half of the batter into greased 1½-quart baking dish; sprinkle with 1 cup cubed Cheddar or Swiss cheese. Pour remaining batter over cheese; stir gently to blend. Let rise and bake as directed above.

Whole Wheat Casserole Bread

Prepare batter as directed for Quick Casserole Bread using 1½ cups all-purpose flour and 1 cup whole wheat flour, and substituting honey for sugar. Let rise and bake as directed above.

Oatmeal Casserole Bread

Prepare batter as directed for Quick Casserole Bread using 1¾ cups flour and 1 cup uncooked quick or old-fashioned oats. Let rise and bake as directed above. Sprinkle with additional oats before baking, if desired.

RED PEPPER BREAD
Makes 1 large loaf or 2 small loaves

2 to 2½ cups all-purpose
   flour, divided

1 cup whole wheat flour

2 tablespoons grated
   Parmesan cheese

1 teaspoon dried rosemary,
   plus additional
   for topping

1 package (¼ ounce)
   instant yeast

½ teaspoon salt

¼ teaspoon dried thyme
   leaves

1¼ cups hot water (130°F)

1 tablespoon olive or
   vegetable oil

½ cup chopped roasted
   red pepper

1 egg white, beaten

2 teaspoons water

1 Combine 1 cup all-purpose flour, whole wheat flour, cheese, 1 teaspoon rosemary, yeast, salt and thyme in large bowl. Stir in 1¼ cups hot water and oil until mixture is smooth. Stir in roasted pepper. Stir in enough remaining all-purpose flour to form soft dough.

2 Turn out dough onto lightly floured surface; flatten slightly. Knead gently 2 to 3 minutes or until smooth and elastic, adding additional all-purpose flour to prevent sticking, if necessary. Place dough in large greased bowl; turn to grease top. Cover and let rise in warm place 30 minutes or until doubled in size.

3 Line baking sheet with parchment paper. Punch down dough. Shape dough into one large or two small round loaves on prepared baking sheet. Cover and let rise 30 minutes or until doubled in size.

4 Preheat oven to 375°F. Slash top of dough with sharp knife. Beat egg white and 2 teaspoons water in small bowl; brush over dough. Sprinkle with additional rosemary, if desired.

5 Bake 35 to 40 minutes for one large loaf, 25 to 30 minutes for two small loaves or until bread is golden and sounds hollow when gently tapped. Cool completely on wire rack.

OATMEAL HONEY BREAD
Makes 1 loaf

1½ to 2 cups all-purpose flour

1 cup plus 1 tablespoon old-fashioned oats, divided

½ cup whole wheat flour

1 package (¼ ounce) instant yeast

1 teaspoon salt

1⅓ cups plus 1 tablespoon water, divided

¼ cup honey

2 tablespoons butter

1 egg

1 Combine 1½ cups all-purpose flour, 1 cup oats, whole wheat flour, yeast and salt in large bowl of stand mixer.

2 Combine 1⅓ cups water, honey and butter in small saucepan; heat over low heat until honey dissolves and butter melts. Let cool to 130°F (temperature of very hot tap water). Add to flour mixture; beat with paddle attachment at medium speed 2 minutes. Add additional all-purpose flour by tablespoonfuls until dough begins to cling together. Dough should be shaggy and very sticky, not dry. (Dough should not form a ball and/or clean side of bowl.)

3 Replace paddle attachment with dough hook; mix at low speed 4 minutes. Place dough in greased bowl; turn to grease top. Cover and let rise in warm place 45 minutes or until doubled in size.

4 Spray 8×4-inch loaf pan with nonstick cooking spray. Punch down dough; turn out onto floured surface. Flatten and stretch dough into 8-inch-long oval. Bring long sides together and pinch to seal; fold over short ends and pinch to seal. Place dough seam side down in prepared pan. Cover and let rise in warm place 20 to 30 minutes or until dough reaches top of pan.

5 Preheat oven to 375°F. Beat egg and remaining 1 tablespoon water in small bowl. Brush top of loaf with egg mixture; sprinkle with remaining 1 tablespoon oats.

6 Bake 30 to 35 minutes or until bread sounds hollow when tapped (190°F on instant-read thermometer). Cool in pan 10 minutes; remove to wire rack to cool completely.

QUATTRO FORMAGGIO FOCACCIA

Makes 12 servings

1 tablespoon sugar

1 package (¼ ounce) instant yeast

1¼ cups warm water (100° to 105°F)

3 to 3¼ cups all-purpose flour

¼ cup plus 2 tablespoons olive oil, divided

1 teaspoon salt

¼ cup marinara sauce with basil

1 cup (4 ounces) shredded Italian cheese blend

1 Dissolve sugar and yeast in warm water in large bowl of stand mixer; let stand 5 minutes or until bubbly. Stir in 3 cups flour, ¼ cup oil and salt with spoon or spatula to form rough dough. Mix with dough hook at low speed 5 minutes, adding additional flour, 1 tablespoon at a time, if necessary for dough to come together. (Dough will be sticky and will not clean side of bowl.)

2 Shape dough into a ball. Place dough in large greased bowl; turn to grease top. Cover and let rise in warm place 1 to 1½ hours or until doubled in size.

3 Punch down dough. Pour remaining 2 tablespoons oil into 13×9-inch baking pan; pat and stretch dough to fill pan. Make indentations in top of dough with fingertips.

4 Spread marinara sauce evenly over dough; sprinkle with cheese. Cover and let rise in warm place 30 minutes or until puffy. Preheat oven to 425°F.

5 Bake 17 to 20 minutes or until golden brown. Cut into squares or strips.

THREE-GRAIN BREAD
Makes 1 loaf

1 cup whole wheat flour

¾ cup all-purpose flour

1 package (¼ ounce) instant yeast

1 cup milk

2 tablespoons honey

1 tablespoon olive oil

1 teaspoon salt

½ cup plus 1 tablespoon old-fashioned oats, divided

¼ cup whole grain cornmeal

1 egg

1 tablespoon water

1 Combine whole wheat flour, all-purpose flour and yeast in large bowl of stand mixer. Combine milk, honey, oil and salt in small saucepan; heat over low heat until warm (110° to 120°F). Add to flour mixture; beat with paddle attachment at medium-high speed 3 minutes. Add ½ cup oats and cornmeal; beat at low speed until blended. If dough is too wet, add additional flour by teaspoonfuls until it begins to come together.

2 Replace paddle attachment with dough hook; mix at low speed 5 minutes or until dough forms a ball. Place dough in large greased bowl; turn to grease top. Cover and let rise in warm place about 1 hour or until dough is puffy and does not spring back when touched.

3 Punch down dough. Shape dough into 8-inch loaf; place on baking sheet lightly sprinkled with cornmeal. Cover and let rise in warm place about 45 minutes or until almost doubled in size. Preheat oven to 375°F.

4 Make shallow slash down center of loaf with sharp knife. Beat egg and water in small bowl; brush lightly over dough. Sprinkle with remaining 1 tablespoon oats.

5 Bake 30 minutes or until bread sounds hollow when tapped (200°F on instant-read thermometer). Remove to wire rack to cool completely.

HEARTY WHOLE WHEAT BREAD
Makes 1 loaf

1 package (¼ ounce)
   active dry yeast
2¼ cups warm water (105°F)
3 cups all-purpose flour
2 cups whole wheat flour
2 teaspoons salt

1 Dissolve yeast in warm water in small bowl; let stand 5 minutes or until bubbly.

2 Combine flours and salt in large bowl; make well in center. Pour in yeast mixture; stir until well blended. Fold, knead and squeeze dough in bowl 2 minutes or until dough comes together (dough will be sticky). Cover and let rise in warm place 1 hour.

3 Gently fold edges of dough in toward center, pressing down lightly to form a ball. Turn dough over; cover and let rise in warm place 3 to 4 hours or until dough has more than doubled in size and is covered with air bubbles.

4 Turn oven to 450°F; place 5- to 6-quart Dutch oven with lid in oven. Preheat oven and pot 30 minutes. Meanwhile, gently ease dough from bowl onto work surface with lightly floured hands, trying not to tear dough as much as possible (do not punch down or flatten dough). Wrap your hands around sides of dough and gently pull it across work surface to form a ball. Repeat until dough is a smooth ball. Lightly dust medium bowl with flour; place dough in bowl. Cover and let rise while oven and pot are heating.

5 Use oven mitts to carefully remove Dutch oven from oven and remove lid (pot and lid will be very hot). Gently turn out dough onto work surface; place in Dutch oven, bottom side up.* Replace lid using oven mitts; return Dutch oven to oven.

6 Bake bread, covered, 30 minutes. Carefully remove lid; bake 10 minutes or until top is deep golden brown. Remove to wire rack to cool completely.

For oval Dutch ovens, gently stretch and shape dough into oval before placing in pot.

SAVORY QUICK BREADS

SHORTCUT BAGELS
Makes 4 servings

1¼ **cups self-rising flour**

1 **cup plain Greek yogurt**

1 **egg, beaten**

Sesame seeds, poppy seeds, dried onion flakes, everything bagel seasoning (optional)

Cream cheese or butter (optional)

1 Preheat oven to 400°F. Line baking sheet with parchment paper.

2 Combine flour and yogurt in large bowl of stand mixer; mix with dough hook at low speed 3 minutes or until well blended.* Turn out dough onto lightly floured surface; knead 2 minutes or until dough is smooth and elastic (dough will be slightly tacky).

3 Shape dough into a ball; cut into quarters. Roll each piece into a ball and poke finger through centers, stretching into bagel shape. (Make large exaggerated loop; it will close up while baking.)

4 Place bagels on prepared baking sheet; brush with egg and sprinkle with desired toppings.

5 Bake 15 to 20 minutes or until lightly browned. Serve warm with cream cheese, if desired.

Or, use heavy spatula to mix dough by hand.

CHEDDAR BISCUITS
Makes 15 biscuits

2 cups all-purpose flour

1 tablespoon sugar

1 tablespoon baking powder

2¼ teaspoons garlic powder, divided

¾ teaspoon plus pinch of salt, divided

1 cup whole milk

½ cup (1 stick) plus 3 tablespoons butter, melted, divided

2 cups (8 ounces) shredded Cheddar cheese

½ teaspoon dried parsley flakes

1 Preheat oven to 450°F. Line baking sheet with parchment paper.

2 Combine flour, sugar, baking powder, 2 teaspoons garlic powder and ¾ teaspoon salt in large bowl; mix well. Add milk and ½ cup melted butter; stir just until dry ingredients are moistened. Stir in cheese just until blended. Drop scant ¼ cupfuls of dough about 1½ inches apart onto prepared baking sheet.

3 Bake 10 to 12 minutes or until golden brown.

4 Meanwhile, combine remaining 3 tablespoons melted butter, ¼ teaspoon garlic powder, pinch of salt and parsley flakes in small bowl; brush over biscuits immediately after removing from oven. Serve warm.

SIMPLE GOLDEN CORN BREAD

Makes 9 to 12 servings

1¼ cups all-purpose flour

¾ cup yellow cornmeal

⅓ cup sugar

2 teaspoons baking powder

1 teaspoon salt

1¼ cups whole milk

¼ cup (½ stick) butter, melted

1 egg

Honey Butter (recipe follows, optional)

1 Preheat oven to 400°F. Spray 8-inch square baking pan with nonstick cooking spray.

2 Combine flour, cornmeal, sugar, baking powder and salt in large bowl; mix well. Whisk milk, butter and egg in medium bowl until well blended. Add to flour mixture; stir just until dry ingredients are moistened. Pour batter into prepared pan.

3 Bake 25 minutes or until golden brown and toothpick inserted into center comes out clean. Prepare Honey Butter, if desired. Serve with corn bread.

Honey Butter

Beat 6 tablespoons (¾ stick) softened butter and ¼ cup honey in medium bowl with electric mixer at medium-high speed until light and creamy.

BACON, ONION AND PARMESAN MUFFINS
Makes 12 muffins

6 slices bacon, chopped

2 cups chopped onions

3 teaspoons sugar, divided

¼ teaspoon dried thyme

1½ cups all-purpose flour

¾ cup grated Parmesan cheese

2 teaspoons baking powder

½ teaspoon salt

¾ cup lager or other light-colored beer

2 eggs

¼ cup extra virgin olive oil

1 Preheat oven to 375°F. Spray 12 standard (2½-inch) muffin cups with nonstick cooking spray.*

2 Cook bacon in large skillet over medium heat until crisp, stirring occasionally. Drain on paper towel-lined plate. Add onions, 1 teaspoon sugar and thyme to skillet; cook 12 minutes or until onions are golden brown, stirring occasionally. Cool 5 minutes; stir in bacon.

3 Combine flour, cheese, baking powder, salt and remaining 2 teaspoons sugar in large bowl; mix well. Whisk lager, eggs and oil in medium bowl until well blended. Add to flour mixture; stir just until dry ingredients are moistened. Gently stir in onion mixture. Spoon batter evenly into prepared muffin cups.

4 Bake 15 minutes or until toothpick inserted into centers comes out clean. Cool in pan 5 minutes; remove to wire rack. Serve warm.

Or grease muffin cups with some of bacon drippings.

EASY CHEESY BUBBLE LOAF
Makes 1 loaf

2 packages (12 ounces each) refrigerated buttermilk biscuits (10 biscuits per package)

2 tablespoons butter, melted

1½ cups (6 ounces) shredded Italian cheese blend

1 Preheat oven to 350°F. Spray 9×5-inch loaf pan with nonstick cooking spray.

2 Separate biscuits; cut each biscuit into four pieces with scissors. Layer half of biscuit pieces in prepared pan. Drizzle with 1 tablespoon butter; sprinkle with 1 cup cheese. Top with remaining biscuit pieces, 1 tablespoon butter and ½ cup cheese.

3 Bake 25 minutes or until golden brown. Serve warm.

 Tip

It's easy to change up the flavors in this simple bread. Try Mexican cheese blend instead of Italian, and add taco seasoning mix and/or hot pepper sauce to the melted butter before drizzling it over the dough. Or, sprinkle ¼ cup chopped ham, salami or crumbled crisp-cooked bacon between the layers of dough.

CONFETTI SCONES
Makes 24 scones

1 tablespoon olive oil

⅓ cup minced red
    bell pepper

⅓ cup minced green
    bell pepper

½ teaspoon dried thyme

1 cup all-purpose flour

¼ cup whole wheat flour

1½ teaspoons baking powder

½ teaspoon baking soda

½ teaspoon sugar

¼ teaspoon salt

¼ teaspoon ground
    red pepper

⅓ cup sour cream

⅓ cup milk

¼ cup grated Parmesan
    cheese

2 tablespoons minced
    green onion

1 Preheat oven to 400°F. Line baking sheets with parchment paper.

2 Heat oil in small skillet over medium heat. Add bell peppers and thyme; cook and stir 5 minutes or until tender.

3 Combine all-purpose flour, whole wheat flour, baking powder, baking soda, sugar, salt and ground red pepper in large bowl; mix well. Add sour cream, milk, cheese, green onion and bell pepper mixture; stir just until sticky dough forms. Drop dough by rounded tablespoonfuls onto prepared baking sheets.

4 Place baking sheets in oven; *immediately reduce heat to 375°F.* Bake 13 to 15 minutes or until golden brown. Remove to wire racks to cool completely.

SWEET POTATO BISCUITS
Makes about 12 biscuits

2½ cups all-purpose flour

¼ cup packed brown sugar

1 tablespoon baking powder

¾ teaspoon salt

¾ teaspoon ground cinnamon

¼ teaspoon ground ginger

¼ teaspoon ground allspice

½ cup cold shortening, cut into small pieces

½ cup chopped pecans

¾ cup mashed canned sweet potatoes

½ cup milk

1 Preheat oven to 450°F.

2 Combine flour, brown sugar, baking powder, salt, cinnamon, ginger and allspice in large bowl; mix well. Cut in shortening with pastry blender or two knives until mixture resembles coarse crumbs. Stir in pecans.

3 Whisk sweet potatoes and milk in small bowl until smooth. Stir into flour mixture until soft dough forms.

4 Turn out dough onto lightly floured surface; knead lightly. Roll out dough to ½-inch thickness. Cut out biscuits with 2½-inch round cutter. Place on ungreased baking sheet.

5 Bake 12 to 14 minutes or until golden brown. Serve warm.

CHEDDAR QUICK BREAD
Makes 1 loaf

2 cups all-purpose flour

4 teaspoons baking powder

1 tablespoon sugar

½ teaspoon salt

½ teaspoon onion powder

½ to 1 teaspoon dry mustard

1½ cups (6 ounces) grated
   Cheddar cheese

1 cup milk

1 egg

2 tablespoons butter, melted

1 Preheat oven to 350°F. Spray 8×4-inch loaf pan with nonstick cooking spray.

2 Combine flour, baking powder, sugar, salt, onion powder and mustard in large bowl; mix well. Stir in cheese until well blended.

3 Whisk milk, egg and butter in medium bowl until well blended. Add to flour mixture; stir just until combined. Spread batter in prepared pan.

4 Bake 40 to 45 minutes or until toothpick inserted into center comes out clean. Cool in pan 10 minutes; remove to wire rack. Serve warm or cool completely.

Tips

Use slices of this bread instead of traditional white bread for grilled cheese sandwiches to make them extra cheesy. For a spicier bread, add ¼ to ½ teaspoon ground red pepper to the dry ingredients.

GARDEN VEGETABLE MUFFINS

Makes 12 muffins

2 cups all-purpose flour

2 tablespoons sugar

1 tablespoon baking powder

¼ teaspoon salt

3 ounces cream cheese,
   cut into small pieces

¾ cup milk

½ cup finely shredded
   or grated carrots

¼ cup chopped green onions

¼ cup vegetable oil

1 egg

1 Preheat oven to 400°F. Line 12 standard (2½-inch) muffin cups with paper baking cups or spray with nonstick cooking spray.

2 Combine flour, sugar, baking powder and salt in large bowl; mix well. Cut in cream cheese with pastry blender or two knives until mixture resembles coarse crumbs.

3 Whisk milk, carrots, green onions, oil and egg in small bowl until blended. Add to flour mixture; stir just until dry ingredients are moistened. Spoon batter evenly into prepared muffin cups.

4 Bake 25 to 30 minutes until toothpick inserted into centers comes out clean. Remove to wire rack to cool 10 minutes. Serve warm.

ROSEMARY PARMESAN BISCUIT POPPERS

Makes 24 small biscuits

2¼ cups biscuit baking mix

⅔ cup milk

⅓ cup grated Parmesan cheese, divided

1 tablespoon chopped fresh rosemary *or* 1 teaspoon dried rosemary, crumbled

1 tablespoon grated lemon peel

⅛ teaspoon ground red pepper

3 tablespoons olive oil

⅛ to ¼ teaspoon coarse salt (optional)

1 Preheat oven to 450°F. Line large baking sheet with parchment paper or spray with nonstick cooking spray.

2 Combine biscuit mix, milk, ¼ cup cheese, rosemary, lemon peel and red pepper in medium bowl; mix well.

3 Drop dough by teaspoonfuls into 1-inch mounds on prepared baking sheet. Sprinkle with remaining cheese.

4 Bake 8 to 10 minutes or until golden brown. Brush biscuits with oil; sprinkle with salt, if desired. Serve immediately.

BROWN SODA BREAD
Makes 1 loaf

2 cups all-purpose flour, plus additional for top of loaf

1 cup whole wheat flour

1 teaspoon baking soda

½ teaspoon salt

½ teaspoon ground ginger

1¼ to 1½ cups buttermilk

3 tablespoons dark molasses (preferably blackstrap)

1 Preheat oven to 375°F. Line baking sheet with parchment paper.

2 Combine 2 cups all-purpose flour, whole wheat flour, baking soda, salt and ginger in large bowl; mix well. Whisk 1¼ cups buttermilk and molasses in medium bowl until well blended. Stir into flour mixture. Add additional buttermilk, 1 tablespoon at a time, if necessary, to make dry, rough dough.

3 Turn out dough onto floured surface; knead 8 to 10 times or just until smooth. (Do not overknead.) Shape dough into round loaf about 1½ inches thick. Place on prepared baking sheet.

4 Use floured knife to cut halfway through dough, scoring into quarters. Sprinkle top of dough with additional all-purpose flour, if desired.

5 Bake about 35 minutes or until bread sounds hollow when tapped. Remove to wire rack to cool slightly. Serve warm.

SUN-DRIED TOMATO BASIL MUFFINS

Makes 12 muffins

½ cup sun-dried tomatoes (about 12 pieces, not oil-packed)

2 cups all-purpose flour

1 tablespoon baking powder

1½ teaspoons dried basil

½ teaspoon salt

¼ teaspoon black pepper

⅛ teaspoon garlic powder

¾ cup milk

½ cup cottage cheese

1 egg

¼ cup vegetable oil

2 teaspoons minced dried onion

1 Preheat oven to 400°F. Spray 12 standard (2½-inch) muffin cups with nonstick cooking spray or line with paper baking cups.

2 Cover sun-dried tomatoes with hot water in small bowl; let stand 10 minutes to soften. Drain and finely chop.

3 Combine flour, baking powder, basil, salt, pepper and garlic powder in large bowl; mix well. Whisk milk, cottage cheese, egg, oil, onion and tomatoes in medium bowl until well blended. Add to flour mixture; stir just until dry ingredients are moistened. Spoon batter evenly into prepared muffin cups.

4 Bake 20 to 25 minutes or until toothpick inserted into centers comes out clean. Cool in pan 5 minutes. Serve warm.

YOGURT CHIVE BISCUITS

Makes 12 biscuits

2 cups all-purpose flour

1 tablespoon sugar

2 teaspoons baking powder

½ teaspoon baking soda

½ teaspoon salt

¼ teaspoon dried oregano

¼ cup (½ stick) cold butter, cut into small pieces

⅔ cup plain Greek yogurt

½ cup milk

¼ cup sour cream

½ cup finely chopped fresh chives

1 Preheat oven to 400°F. Line baking sheet with parchment paper.

2 Combine flour, sugar, baking powder, baking soda, salt and oregano in large bowl; mix well. Cut in butter with pastry blender or two knives until coarse crumbs form. Add yogurt, milk and sour cream; stir gently to form soft sticky dough. Stir in chives.

3 Drop dough by ¼ cupfuls 1½ inches apart onto prepared baking sheet.

4 Bake 15 to 16 minutes or until golden brown. Remove to wire rack to cool slightly. Serve warm.

BROCCOLI CHEESE SCONES

Makes 16 scones

2½ cups all-purpose flour

1 tablespoon baking powder

1 tablespoon sugar

2 teaspoons salt

½ teaspoon red pepper flakes

1 cup broccoli florets

½ cup (1 stick) cold butter, cut into small pieces

1½ cups (6 ounces) shredded Cheddar cheese

1 cup milk

1 Preheat oven to 400°F. Line baking sheets with parchment paper.

2 Combine flour, baking powder, sugar, salt and red pepper flakes in food processor; process 10 seconds. Add broccoli and butter; process until mixture forms coarse meal, scraping down side of bowl once.

3 Transfer mixture to large bowl. Add cheese and milk; stir until blended. Knead gently to form dough.

4 Divide dough in half. Press one half of dough into 8-inch circle on cutting board. Cut into eight wedges; place on prepared baking sheet. Repeat with remaining half of dough.

5 Bake 15 to 20 minutes or until lightly browned.

SMALL BREADS

PITA BREAD
Makes 8 pita breads

3½ cups all-purpose flour

1 tablespoon salt

1 tablespoon sugar

1 package (¼ ounce) instant yeast

1½ cups warm water (120°F)

2 tablespoons olive oil

1 Combine flour, salt, sugar and yeast in large bowl; mix well. Add 1½ cups water and oil; stir with wooden spoon until rough dough forms. If dough appears too dry, add additional 1 to 2 tablespoons water. Knead on lightly floured surface 5 to 7 minutes or until dough is smooth and elastic. Or knead with electric mixer using dough hook at low speed 5 minutes.

2 Shape dough into a ball. Place dough in greased bowl; turn to grease top. Cover and let rise in warm place 1 hour or until doubled in size.

3 Preheat oven to 500°F. Turn out dough onto lightly floured surface; press into circle. Cut dough into eight wedges. Roll each wedge into a smooth ball; flatten slightly. Let rest 10 minutes.

4 Roll out each ball into circle about ¼ inch thick. Place on two ungreased baking sheets.

5 Bake one baking sheet at a time 5 minutes or until pitas are puffed and set. Remove to wire rack to cool slightly.

PULL-APART RYE ROLLS
Makes 24 rolls

¾ cup water

2 tablespoons butter

2 tablespoons molasses

2¼ cups all-purpose flour, divided

½ cup rye flour

⅓ cup nonfat dry milk powder

1 package (¼ ounce) active dry yeast

1½ teaspoons salt

1½ teaspoons caraway seeds

2 teaspoons vegetable oil

1 Combine water, butter and molasses in small saucepan; heat over low heat to 120°F. Combine 1¼ cups all-purpose flour, rye flour, milk powder, yeast, salt and caraway seeds in large bowl of stand mixer. Slowly add water mixture; beat with paddle attachment at low speed to form soft, sticky dough.

2 Replace paddle attachment with dough hook. Slowly add enough additional all-purpose flour, about ¾ cup, to form rough dough. Add remaining flour, 1 tablespoon at a time, if necessary to prevent sticking. Mix at low speed 5 minutes or until dough is smooth and elastic.

3 Shape dough into a ball. Place dough in greased bowl; turn to grease top. Cover and let rise in warm place 35 to 40 minutes or until dough has increased in size by one third.

4 Spray 8- or 9-inch round cake pan with nonstick cooking spray. Punch down dough. Divide dough in half; roll each half into 12-inch log. Cut each log into 12 pieces with sharp knife; shape each piece into a tight ball. Place balls in single layer in prepared pan; brush with oil. Cover loosely with lightly greased sheet of plastic wrap; let rise in warm place 45 minutes or until doubled in size. Preheat oven to 375°F.

5 Bake 15 to 20 minutes or until golden brown. Cool in pan 5 minutes; remove to wire rack to cool completely.

PESTO-PARMESAN TWISTS
Makes 24 breadsticks

1 loaf (1 pound) frozen bread dough, thawed according to package directions

¼ cup pesto sauce

⅔ cup grated Parmesan cheese, divided

1 tablespoon olive oil

1 Line baking sheets with parchment paper.

2 Roll out dough into 20×10-inch rectangle on lightly floured surface. Spread pesto evenly over half of dough; sprinkle with ⅓ cup cheese. Fold remaining half of dough over filling, forming 10-inch square.

3 Roll square into 12×10-inch rectangle. Cut into 12 (1-inch) strips with sharp knife. Cut strips in half crosswise to form 24 strips total. Twist each strip several times; place on prepared baking sheets. Cover with plastic wrap; let rise in warm place 20 minutes.

4 Preheat oven to 350°F. Brush breadsticks with oil; sprinkle with remaining ⅓ cup cheese.

5 Bake 16 to 18 minutes or until golden brown. Serve warm.

DINNER ROLLS
Makes 12 rolls

½ cup plus 2 tablespoons milk

¼ cup shortening

2 to 2¼ cups all-purpose flour, divided

2 tablespoons sugar

1 package (¼ ounce) active dry yeast

½ teaspoon salt

1 egg

1 Combine milk and shortening in small saucepan; heat over low heat to 110° to 120°F (shortening does not need to melt completely).

2 Combine ¾ cup flour, sugar, yeast and salt in large bowl of stand mixer. Slowly add milk mixture; mix with paddle attachment at low speed until well blended. Add egg and ½ cup flour; beat at medium speed 2 minutes. Beat in enough additional flour, ½ to ¾ cup, to form soft dough.

3 Replace paddle attachment with dough hook. Add remaining flour, 1 tablespoon at a time, if necessary to prevent sticking. Mix at low speed 5 to 7 minutes or until dough is smooth and elastic.

4 Shape dough into a ball. Place dough in greased bowl; turn to grease top. Cover and let rise in warm place 1 hour or until doubled in size.

5 Punch down dough; knead on lightly floured surface 1 minute. Cover and let rest 10 minutes. Spray 8-inch square baking pan with nonstick cooking spray. Cut dough into 12 pieces. Shape each piece of dough into a ball; place in rows in prepared pan. Cover and let rise in warm place 30 minutes or until doubled in size. Preheat oven to 375°F.

6 Bake 15 to 20 minutes or until golden brown. Remove to wire rack to cool slightly. Serve warm.

GARLIC KNOTS
Makes 20 knots

1 package (¼ ounce)
  active dry yeast

1 teaspoon sugar

¾ cup warm water
  (105° to 115°F)

2¼ cups all-purpose flour

2 tablespoons olive oil,
  divided

1½ teaspoons salt, divided

4 tablespoons (½ stick)
  butter, divided

1 tablespoon minced garlic

¼ teaspoon garlic powder

½ cup grated Parmesan
  cheese

2 tablespoons chopped
  fresh parsley

½ teaspoon dried oregano

1 Dissolve yeast and sugar in warm water in large bowl of stand mixer; let stand 5 minutes or until bubbly. Add flour, 1 tablespoon oil and 1 teaspoon salt; mix with dough hook at low speed 5 minutes or until dough is smooth and elastic.

2 Shape dough into a ball. Place dough in greased bowl; turn to grease top. Cover and let rise in warm place 1 hour or until doubled in size.

3 Melt 2 tablespoons butter in small saucepan over low heat. Add remaining 1 tablespoon oil, ½ teaspoon salt, minced garlic and garlic powder; cook over very low heat 5 minutes. Pour into small bowl; set aside.

4 Preheat oven to 400°F. Line baking sheet with parchment paper.

5 Punch down dough. Turn out dough onto lightly floured surface; let rest 10 minutes. Roll out dough into 10×8-inch rectangle; cut into 20 (2-inch) squares. Roll each piece into 8-inch rope; tie in a knot. Place knots on prepared baking sheet; brush with butter mixture.

6 Bake 10 minutes or until lightly browned. Meanwhile, melt remaining 2 tablespoons butter. Combine cheese, parsley and oregano in small bowl; mix well. Brush melted butter over knots immediately after baking; sprinkle with cheese mixture. Cool slightly; serve warm.

BEER PRETZEL ROLLS
Makes 12 rolls

1¼ cups lager or pale ale,
    at room temperature

3 tablespoons packed
    brown sugar

2 tablespoons milk

2 tablespoons butter, melted

1 package (¼ ounce)
    instant yeast

3 to 4 cups bread flour,
    divided

2 teaspoons salt

4 quarts water

½ cup baking soda

2 teaspoons coarse salt

1 Combine lager, brown sugar, milk, butter and yeast in large bowl of stand mixer. Add 1 cup flour and 2 teaspoons salt; beat with paddle attachment at low speed 2 minutes.

2 Replace paddle attachment with dough hook. Add enough remaining flour, ½ cup at a time, to form stiff dough that cleans side of bowl. Mix at low speed about 5 minutes or until dough is smooth and elastic. Shape dough into a ball. Place dough in greased bowl; turn to grease top. Cover and let rise in warm place 1 hour or until doubled in size.

3 Turn out dough onto lightly floured surface; knead several times. Divide dough into 12 pieces; shape each piece into a smooth ball by gently pulling top surface to underside and pinching bottom to seal. Place on ungreased baking sheet. Cover and let rise in warm place 30 minutes or until doubled in size.

4 Position oven rack in center of oven. Preheat oven to 425°F. Line second baking sheet with parchment paper.

5 Bring water and baking soda to a boil in large saucepan over high heat. Add rolls to water, a few at a time; cook until puffed, turning once. Drain rolls on clean kitchen towel; place 2 inches apart on prepared baking sheet. Cut 1½-inch "X" in top of each roll with kitchen scissors. Sprinkle with coarse salt.

6 Bake 15 to 18 minutes or until crisp and deep golden brown. Remove to wire rack to cool slightly.

SPANIKOPITA PULL-APARTS
Makes 24 rolls

4 tablespoons (½ stick) butter, melted, divided

12 frozen white dinner rolls (⅓ of 3-pound package),* thawed according to package directions

1 package (10 ounces) frozen chopped spinach, thawed and squeezed dry

4 green onions, finely chopped (about ¼ cup packed)

1 clove garlic, minced

1 teaspoon dried dill weed

½ teaspoon salt

⅛ teaspoon black pepper

1 cup (4 ounces) crumbled feta cheese

¾ cup (3 ounces) grated Monterey Jack cheese, divided

If frozen dinner rolls are not available, substitute one 16-ounce loaf of frozen bread dough or pizza dough. Thaw according to package directions and divide into 12 pieces.

1 Brush large (10-inch) ovenproof skillet with ½ tablespoon butter. Cut rolls in half to make 24 balls of dough.

2 Combine spinach, green onions, garlic, dill weed, salt and pepper in medium bowl; mix well to break apart spinach. Add feta, ½ cup Monterey Jack and remaining 3½ tablespoons butter; mix well.

3 Coat each ball of dough with spinach mixture; arrange in single layer in prepared skillet. Sprinkle any remaining spinach mixture between and over balls of dough. Cover and let rise in warm place about 40 minutes or until almost doubled in size.

4 Preheat oven to 350°F. Sprinkle remaining ¼ cup Monterey Jack over dough.

5 Bake 35 to 40 minutes or until golden brown. Serve warm.

PROSCIUTTO PROVOLONE ROLLS
Makes 12 rolls

3 cups all-purpose flour, divided

1 package (¼ ounce) instant yeast

1½ teaspoons salt

1 cup warm water (120°F)

2 tablespoons olive oil

⅓ cup garlic and herb spreadable cheese

6 thin slices prosciutto (3-ounce package)

6 slices (1 ounce each) provolone cheese

1 Combine 1½ cups flour, yeast and salt in large bowl of stand mixer. Add warm water and oil; beat with paddle attachment at medium speed 2 minutes.

2 Replace paddle attachment with dough hook. Add remaining 1½ cups flour; mix at low speed 2 minutes to form soft dough that cleans side of bowl. Mix at low speed 6 to 8 minutes or until dough is smooth and elastic.

3 Shape dough into a ball. Place dough in greased bowl; turn to grease top. Cover and let rise in warm place about 30 minutes or until doubled in size.

4 Punch down dough. Spray 12 standard (2½-inch) muffin cups with nonstick cooking spray.

5 Roll out dough into 12×10-inch rectangle on lightly floured surface. Spread garlic and herb cheese evenly over dough; top with prosciutto and provolone slices. Starting with long side, roll up dough jelly-roll style; pinch seam to seal. Cut crosswise into 1-inch slices; arrange slices, cut sides up, in prepared muffin cups. Cover and let rise in warm place about 25 minutes or until almost doubled in size. Preheat oven to 375°F.

6 Bake about 20 minutes or until golden brown. Loosen edges of rolls with knife; remove to wire rack. Serve warm.

SOFT GARLIC BREADSTICKS

Makes about 16 breadsticks

1½ cups water

6 tablespoons (¾ stick) butter, divided

4 cups all-purpose flour

2 tablespoons sugar

1 package (¼ ounce) active dry yeast

1½ teaspoons salt

¾ teaspoon coarse salt

¼ teaspoon garlic powder

1 Heat water and 2 tablespoons butter in small saucepan or microwavable bowl to 110° to 115°F. (Butter does not need to melt completely.)

2 Combine flour, sugar, yeast and 1½ teaspoons salt in large bowl of stand mixer. Add water mixture; mix with dough hook at low speed until dough begins to come together. Mix about 5 minutes or until dough is smooth and elastic.

3 Shape dough into a ball. Place dough in greased bowl; turn to grease top. Cover and let rise in warm place about 1 hour or until doubled in size.

4 Line two baking sheets with parchment paper or spray with nonstick cooking spray. Punch down dough. For each breadstick, pull off piece of dough slightly larger than a golf ball (about 2 ounces) and roll between hands or on work surface into 7-inch-long rope. Place on prepared baking sheets; cover loosely and let rise in warm place about 45 minutes or until doubled in size.

5 Preheat oven to 400°F. Melt remaining 4 tablespoons butter. Brush breadsticks with half of melted butter; sprinkle with coarse salt.

6 Bake breadsticks 13 to 15 minutes or until golden brown. Stir garlic powder into remaining melted butter; brush over breadsticks immediately after removing from oven. Serve warm.

HERBED POTATO ROLLS
Makes 12 rolls

2¾ cups bread flour, divided

½ cup instant potato flakes

1 tablespoon sugar

1 package (¼ ounce) instant yeast

1¼ teaspoons dried rosemary

1 teaspoon salt

¼ teaspoon black pepper

1 cup warm milk (120°F)

1½ tablespoons olive oil

1 egg, beaten

Poppy seeds, sesame seeds and/or additional dried rosemary (optional)

1 Combine 1 cup flour, potato flakes, sugar, yeast, rosemary, salt and pepper in large bowl of stand mixer. Add milk and oil; beat with paddle attachment at medium speed 2 minutes.

2 Replace paddle attachment with dough hook; mix in enough remaining flour to form soft dough. Mix at medium-low speed 6 to 8 minutes or until dough is smooth and elastic.

3 Shape dough into a ball. Place dough in greased bowl; turn to grease top. Cover and let rise in warm place about 20 minutes or until doubled in size.

4 Line baking sheet with parchment paper. Punch down dough. Divided dough into 12 pieces; roll each piece into 10-inch rope on lightly floured surface. Shape rope into a coil, tucking end under coil. Place 2 inches apart on prepared baking sheet. Cover and let rise in warm place about 40 minutes or until doubled in size.

5 Preheat oven to 375°F. Brush rolls with beaten egg; sprinkle with toppings, if desired.

6 Bake about 18 minutes or until golden brown. Remove to wire rack. Serve warm or at room temperature.

METRIC CONVERSION CHART

VOLUME MEASUREMENTS (dry)

1/8 teaspoon = 0.5 mL
1/4 teaspoon = 1 mL
1/2 teaspoon = 2 mL
3/4 teaspoon = 4 mL
1 teaspoon = 5 mL
1 tablespoon = 15 mL
2 tablespoons = 30 mL
1/4 cup = 60 mL
1/3 cup = 75 mL
1/2 cup = 125 mL
2/3 cup = 150 mL
3/4 cup = 175 mL
1 cup = 250 mL
2 cups = 1 pint = 500 mL
3 cups = 750 mL
4 cups = 1 quart = 1 L

VOLUME MEASUREMENTS (fluid)

1 fluid ounce (2 tablespoons) = 30 mL
4 fluid ounces (1/2 cup) = 125 mL
8 fluid ounces (1 cup) = 250 mL
12 fluid ounces (1 1/2 cups) = 375 mL
16 fluid ounces (2 cups) = 500 mL

WEIGHTS (mass)

1/2 ounce = 15 g
1 ounce = 30 g
3 ounces = 90 g
4 ounces = 120 g
8 ounces = 225 g
10 ounces = 285 g
12 ounces = 360 g
16 ounces = 1 pound = 450 g

DIMENSIONS

1/16 inch = 2 mm
1/8 inch = 3 mm
1/4 inch = 6 mm
1/2 inch = 1.5 cm
3/4 inch = 2 cm
1 inch = 2.5 cm

OVEN TEMPERATURES

250°F = 120°C
275°F = 140°C
300°F = 150°C
325°F = 160°C
350°F = 180°C
375°F = 190°C
400°F = 200°C
425°F = 220°C
450°F = 230°C

BAKING PAN SIZES

Utensil	Size in Inches/Quarts	Metric Volume	Size in Centimeters
Baking or Cake Pan (square or rectangular)	8×8×2	2 L	20×20×5
	9×9×2	2.5 L	23×23×5
	12×8×2	3 L	30×20×5
	13×9×2	3.5 L	33×23×5
Loaf Pan	8×4×3	1.5 L	20×10×7
	9×5×3	2 L	23×13×7
Round Layer Cake Pan	8×1 1/2	1.2 L	20×4
	9×1 1/2	1.5 L	23×4
Pie Plate	8×1 1/4	750 mL	20×3
	9×1 1/4	1 L	23×3
Baking Dish or Casserole	1 quart	1 L	—
	1 1/2 quart	1.5 L	—
	2 quart	2 L	—